ALONE
With
The
ALONE

AN EIGHT-DAY RETREAT:

ALONE
With
The
ALONE

George A. Maloney, SJ

CONTEMPLATIVE MINISTRIES
850 COASTLINE DRIVE
SEAL BEACH, CA 90740

Imprimi Potest: Rev. Vincent M. Cooke, S.J.
                   Provincial of the New York Province
                   December 8, 1980

Acknowledgments

Sincere thanks to Mrs. Rita Ruggiero for typing the manuscript
and to Sister Joseph Agnes, S.C.H. and Sister Francoise
O'Hare, R.S.H.M. for their careful reading and correcting of
the manuscript and for other suggestions that proved most
helpful.

Excerpts from THE JERUSALEM BIBLE, copyright © 1966 by
Darton, Longman & Todd and Doubleday & Company, Inc.
Used by permission of the publisher. All scriptural texts are from
this bible version unless otherwise noted.

International Standard Book Number: 0-87793-242-5 (Cloth)
                                    0-87793-243-3 (Paper)

Library of Congress Catalog Card Number: 81-70021

Printed and bound in the United States of America.

Text and cover design: Elizabeth French

First printing, January, 1982
Fifth printing, January, 1987
55,000 copies in print

To Margaret Noe and her eight children, fellow pilgrims on our same journey.

CONTENTS

CONTENTS

FOREWORD

God is doing a wonderful work throughout our land. He is pouring out his Spirit of love in a renewing of Christ's church that is exciting to experience. One evident sign of the outpouring of Jesus' Spirit is the tremendous hunger and thirst among Christians of all churches and of all walks of life for deeper prayer.

Retreat houses all over America are continuously filled as weary pilgrims seek to go aside and rest a while with God. Our modern life is becoming so fast and furious in its pace that we feel torn from our roots. As flotsam tossed to and fro on a stormy ocean, we bob up and down in a fast rip tide of activities that tire us out as we are carried farther away from the shore.

We need to enter into an aloneness with the Alone, with God himself, if we are to find any meaning in our human existence. This is not escapism or avoidance of our responsibility to serve others. It is a movement of the Spirit to contact God and to experience him as the beginning and the end of our lives. As a feverish person on a sick bed cries for water to slake a burning thirst, we crave the experience of God who alone can give direction and purpose to our fragmented lives.

A "Directed" Retreat   Along with our thirst to be alone with God is a similar thirst to listen to God speak to us. He

11

speaks to us in the revealed words of holy scripture. We rightfully fear, however, that when we are alone with God we might create our own idol, the God *we* want to love and serve; in a word, the God we want to manipulate and control in order not to suffer and eventually not to die to our self-centeredness.

How can we listen to God's revelation unless we are rooted in the Christian community that "hands down" the tradition of the "mystery" that St. Paul strove to preach? Yet often Christians serious about their growth in the word of God complain of the lack of solid spiritual directors who are rooted in the true tradition where alone God's word becomes truly salvific and healing.

Many such Christians have discovered how much spiritual direction in God's word can be received in a "directed" retreat. Usually this takes the form of an eight- or 30-day retreat under the guidance of a spiritual (one taught by the Holy Spirit) director. Such a director becomes a channel for the retreatant to experience the saving power of Jesus Christ in his *kairos* action as Christ's mysteries are prayerfully experienced, not as past history, but as the retreatant's present and evolving life of decision before the Trinity.

Guided by the Spirit   It is not always possible to find both the time to make a full, directed retreat and a good director, one who can skillfully and prayerfully guide a person one to one. The Holy Spirit, however, cannot be limited in his riches by our own human contingencies. St. Ignatius understood this in his rules for adapting the *Spiritual Exercises* to the needs of the individual.

He thus encouraged a retreatant who could not give full time to the sole purpose of doing the *Exercises* to make an adapted retreat. Such a retreatant receives from a director the developments of certain meditations and considerations which are to be prayed over at home.

Foreword

Trusting in the power of the Holy Spirit to meet the needs of sincere individuals, I have written this book as an aid to those who desire to make a retreat. If you are able to give a full eight days to being alone in prayer with God, this book is offered to guide you in your prayerful considerations. No book, of course, can replace a skilled, Spirit-filled director, but I hope that you may find it a help on your retreat alone with the Alone.

This book is also intended as an aid to those who cannot pull away from their activities but who would like to make a retreat extended over several weeks or even months. The considerations contained herein need not cover only eight days.

In either case this book of prayerful considerations on the key mysteries of the Christian faith, especially those touching Jesus Christ as found in the gospel narratives, can be of help to anyone seeking some "input" in his or her daily encounter with the Trinity. I have drawn heavily from scripture and the insights from the great mystics of the Christian East.

I pray that these chapters may be an encountering point for you, the reader, to go aside and meet God, Father, Son and Holy Spirit, so that, alone with the Alone, you may never be alone again, but you may always live in an *I-Thou* love relationship with God in their *We* community. May you come from your "retreat" to bring forth a similar community of love with all you meet.

GEORGE A. MALONEY, S.J.

The Call to the Desert

You are ready to begin your retreat. You have been waiting for this moment for a long time. Now the moment is here.

God has been working quietly in the past months to prepare you to hear his call to enter into the darkness of the desert of your heart. How beautifully God has been filling you with a hunger and thirst that you know only he can satisfy. Lately your work with all of its many projects has not been as satisfying to you as before. Perhaps your friends, who before were always there to pick up your spirits when you were lonely, now do not seem to answer all your needs.

> God, you are my God, I am seeking you,
> my soul is thirsting for you,
> my flesh is longing for you,
> a land parched, weary and waterless;
> I long to gaze on you in the Sanctuary,
> and to see your power and glory.
> Your love is better than life itself,
> my lips will recite your praise (Ps 63:1-3).

The thirst to drink of God's living waters, his Spirit of love, has been growing in your heart. Only God will suffice!

> As a doe longs
>   for running streams,
> so longs my soul
>   for you, my God.

ALONE WITH THE ALONE

My soul thirsts for God,
   the God of life,
when shall I go to see
   the face of God?
. . . In the daytime may Yahweh
   command his love to come,
and by night may his song be on my lips,
   a prayer to the God of my life! (Ps 42:1-2,8).

Thirst for God   Such a spiritual thirst is at the heart of being truly human. With St. Augustine, we know in the depths of our being that God has made us for himself and our hearts are restless until they rest in him. It is a "stretching out" to become whole. It is a nostalgia to leave the husks of swine and return home to our heavenly Father. Thirst in the biblical sense is what we experience as we begin to grow in deeper union with God.

How St. Paul burned with a thirst to "put on Christ"! He was ready to consider everything else as dung compared to the joy of being more and more one with Jesus Christ. Jesus invites us all to come to him if we thirst for him.

"If any man is thirsty, let him come to me!
Let the man come and drink who believes in me!" (Jn
   7:37-38).

Jesus is the rock that stands in the desert of our life. He invites us to come and drink of his life-giving Spirit.

You have been thirsting for this water all your life. You have been prayerfully waiting for Jesus to stand and knock at the door of your heart (Rv 3:20).

Prayer—A paradox   Simone Weil has described prayer as a patient waiting with expectancy. It is a paradox of tension that combines the absence and the presence of God; the *already* and the *not yet;* the *returning* and the *going;* tender loving possession and the agony of searching for the lost. Prayer is a call to break the idols of God we have created according to our own self-centered needs. It is to answer God's call to conversion; to purify our hearts from the illusions of immortality, from the belief that we have an eternal beginning and no end and that we justify our own existence in ourselves.

Need of Silence   One of the most needed commodities in modern life—and one which must be a large part of your retreat—is silence. Yet you cannot buy silence. The wealthy can afford to purchase seclusion and avoid the noisy crowds, but silence is more than the absence of noise.

Have you ever found yourself in a still forest where the only sound came from the breeze blowing through the pine trees or an occasional bird call, yet inside you there was much noise? Mentally you were wrestling with a problem and you did not enjoy inner peace.

Perhaps, riding the subway or an airplane, amid much external noise, you have experienced an inner quiet, a silence that was like a calming, creative force flowing over you. It is this type of silence that is so desperately needed in our world today.

The poet Longfellow expressed this experience as an inward stillness:

> Let us, then, labor for an inward stillness—
> An inward stillness and an inward healing;
> That perfect silence where the lips and heart
> Are still, and we no longer entertain
> Our own imperfect thoughts and vain opinions,
> But God alone speaks in us, and we wait
> In singleness of heart, that we may know
> His will, and in silence of our spirits,
> That we may do His will and do that only.

Afraid to be Alone   To enter into our inner being, we

17

must embrace silence. Yet this is a discipline that we find most difficult. We find ourselves resisting at every turn. We will do almost anything to remain "up on surface," in command of our lives by means of our discursive powers. We try to fashion every situation to our own liking. We truly can create our own world. And many times we mistakenly call this our "creative" power!

But in reality it is our power for *undoing* ourselves, for putting off the whole process of becoming the healed, wholly integrated person God knows us to be when from the depths of our being he calls us by our name (Is 43:1). We are masters at avoiding a confrontation with the real person that we are. We can play games, put on masks, become distracted by the words and values of the people around us. We can busy ourselves "saying" prayers; we can even use so-called "silent" prayer to avoid the real silence in which we look at our inner feelings, look at both the light and the darkness that are struggling for possession of us. As long as we indulge in such game-playing, we show that we are afraid to be silent. We fear to look inward and honestly ask for healing from the transcendent God.

The Silence of God

To understand the creative power in silence, we must understand something about God's own silence. God is love, and silence is the perfect communication of the Father and his Son through the Holy Spirit of love. God loves and pours himself completely out into his one Word and this one Word receives the fullness of the Father, not in two words, but in the silence of one Word. St. Paul says, "In him lives the fullness of divinity" (Col 2:9).

God not only speaks his Word in silence from all eternity without any interruption, but he also hears this Word in

18

perfect silence as an echo of his own reflected beauty and love. Through the silent gasp of love that is the Holy Spirit bringing God the Father together with his Son, the heavenly Father hears his Word continually coming back to him in a perfect, eternal "yes" of total, surrendering love that is again the Holy Spirit.

God's Creative Silence in Nature   Through God's one Word, St. John writes in his prologue, all of creation is brought into existence. Mountains and oceans, birds and beasts, flowers and grains tumble forth in profuse richness from the finger tips of the creating God—and all is done in silence! When we can withdraw from our busy, fragmented worlds that pull us into so many directions, filling us with frustrations and anxieties, and enter into God's silence found in all of primeval nature, then we are opening ourselves up to deep healing. When we enter into the primeval, endless *now* of God's quiet, we enter into a state of *being*. It is hardly a state of passivity or idleness. It is beyond pragmatic descriptions. It is where life and love merge into the same experience.

If we wish to encounter God on a deeper level of communication than that of concepts, we must enter into the restful silence of God. We must draw upon the vast richness of solitude that the physical world has to offer. It is at such a time that Pascal cried out, "The eternal silence of those boundless spaces strikes awe into my soul!" When we begin to hear God's love and beauty pouring forth in his silence throughout all of nature, we can pray with St. Augustine:

> Heaven and earth and all that is in the universe cry out to me from all directions that I, O God, must love Thee, and they do not cease to cry out to all so that they have no excuse.

God pulsates with his silent energies in all created nature. Plants, trees, birds and animals cry out unceasingly to us noisy pilgrims along life's highways: "It is in him that we live, and move, and exist" (Ac 17:28). When we become silent we discover God; as Psalm 46:10 puts it, "Pause a while and know that I am God."

God works efficiently throughout all nature and he accomplishes his purpose in silence. The butterfly moves about in silence, telling us of God! The giant sequoia stretches its head toward its maker in silent praise and adoration!

Moments of escape into primeval nature may be rare in our urban living; nevertheless, we need to learn how to turn into our hearts and find God breathing forth his healing love in silence.

A Silenced Heart   We, of all God's creations, have been made according to God's image and likeness (Gn 1:26). Deep down at the core of our innermost being is found the focal point that holy scripture calls the "heart." * It was here that Jesus told us to pray to our heavenly Father:

> "But when you pray, go to your private room and, when you have shut your door, pray to your Father who is in that secret place and your Father who sees all that is done in secret will reward you" (Mt 6:6).

Of all creation God's silence grows deepest and most intense when he communicates with us. God gives himself directly to us in the depths of our beings, in our hearts. He does so in the silence of begetting his Word through the fiery gaze of the Spirit of love. But what a struggle it is for us to become silent before God's silent love! It entails letting go of the control that we have over our lives. It necessitates the death of our false selves in order to find our true selves in the Other dwelling intimately within us.

In the retreat you will struggle to enter into the darkness of faith and there to accept the silent love of the indwelling God. St. Augustine exhorts us, "Enter into

---

* The *heart* in the Old Testament Semitic understanding of the word as symbol meant the deepest reaches of one's inner being where love is generated in self-sacrifice for the one loved.

20

yourself; it is in the interior man where Truth is found." When you have the courage to drop your defenses and sink into the inner darkness, you enter into a new experience of knowing by not knowing. After some experience of praying in silence, without words and masks, you learn to let go. You breathe more deeply, more peacefully. You can go down with ease into your inner self and joyfully stretch out your spiritual hands to grasp God who now is so close to you. It seems that you have been given new, interior eyes that lovingly gaze on him. In that silent gaze you know yourself in God's unique love for you. With new interior ears you ever so quietly listen to God as he communicates himself to you without words, images or forms.

Your prayer in such silence through the deepening of faith infused into you by the Holy Spirit brings with it a great peace because you are touching God who resides at the center of your being. Your prayer is now not something that you do, so much as an entering into a state of being. The Greek word, *enstasis,* a standing inside, best describes the prayer of the heart that unfolds in deep, interior silence. You seem to be standing inside your real self, not outside *(ecstasis),* and inside your deepest reality you are truly centered *in* God. You stand in his holy presence, loving him without words or images or props. The totality of your being is in a tranquil state of loving surrender.

Silence: A Continuing Process of Growth   Silence admits of many degrees. There can be a physical silence outside ourselves. There can be a physical silence in our various members: no speech, controlled moderation of restless members, the hands, feet, etc. There can be various degrees of psychic silence of the emotions, the imagination, the memory, the intellect and the will. But the greatest silence is that of our spirit with God's Spirit. "Heart speaks to heart" in silence, the language of self-surrendering love.

ALONE WITH THE ALONE

This is a state of highest expanded consciousness brought about by the Holy Spirit through an increased infusion of faith, hope and love. It is the Holy Spirit alone who brings forth his gifts and fruits in your relationships with others. Your life, now rooted more deeply in the ultimate, reflects more exactly than at any earlier stage the worth of your prayer life.

Such silence in your spirit is a gift of God's Spirit of love. The Holy Spirit dwelling within you teaches you how to pray deeply in your heart: "The love of God has been poured into our hearts by the Holy Spirit who has been given us" (Rm 5:5). It is God "who gives you his Holy Spirit" (1 Th 4:8). Our bodies through Jesus Christ have become temples of the Holy Spirit (1 Cor 6:19).

Of yourself, you are utterly incapable of praying in silence to God. Such silence is a continued process of letting go and allowing the Holy Spirit to pray within you.

> The Spirit too comes to help us in our weakness. For when we cannot choose words in order to pray properly, the Spirit himself expresses our plea in a way that could never be put into words, and God who knows everything in our hearts knows perfectly well what he means and that the pleas of the saints expressed by the Spirit are according to the mind of God (Rm 8:26-27).

It is the Spirit that gives life (Jn 6:63). The redemptive work of Jesus Christ can be seen as a continued process taking place in the silence of your heart in deep prayer. He is releasing his Holy Spirit within you as he had promised he would (Lk 11:13). The Spirit allows you to transcend the limitations of your words and ideas about God in order to enter into the silent language of love, an experience beyond anything human or controllable. The Spirit of Jesus sent into your heart allows you to know his presence and yield to his love toward the Father and the Son: "You know him because he is with you; he is in you" (Jn 14:17).

22

Praying in the Spirit   What you experience continually when the Spirit prays within you is the utter conviction that you are God's beloved child. God loves you! But the good news that the Holy Spirit breathes forth within your heart through an infused experience is that now you *know* that you *know* God loves you! You can truly cry out: "Abba, Father!" (Rm 8:15; Ga 4:6).

> The proof that you are sons is that God has sent the Spirit of his Son into our hearts: the Spirit that cries, "Abba, Father," and it is this that makes you a son, you are not a slave any more; and if God has made you son, then he has made you heir (Ga 4:6-7).

This Spirit "reaches the depths of everything, even the depths of God" (1 Cor 2:10). It is thus that we are taught by God's very own Spirit of love, making us "spiritual" beings. If in deep, silent prayer we are to touch the very depths of God, this can be done only through his Spirit: "In the same way the depths of God can only be known by the Spirit of God. Now instead of the spirit of the world, we have received the Spirit that comes from God, to teach us to understand the gifts that he has given us. Therefore we teach . . . in the way that the Spirit teaches us; we teach spiritual things spiritually" (1 Cor 2:11-13).

Contemplation   To contemplate is to move beyond your own activity and become activated by the inner power of the Holy Spirit. It means to be swept up into the threefold love current of Father, Son and Holy Spirit. In the silent prayer of the heart, a gift of the Spirit praying within you, you move beyond feelings, emotions, even thoughts. The Spirit is so powerfully operative that imagining or reasoning can only be noise that disturbs the silent communication of God at the core of your being.

If you introduce "noise" by speaking words and fashioning images of God, then you are limiting his freedom to speak his word as he wishes, when he wishes. The Holy Spirit frees you so God can give himself to you. With utter freedom and joy, respond always in deep silence and humble self-surrender to his inner presence.

Silence—The Language of the Innermost Self   One of the outstanding psychiatrists in America today is Dr. Carl Rogers. He speaks of developing our personalities by moving beyond the responses we have developed from our past life-experiences. For him, deep down in each of us is the *innermost self.* This core of personality is basically healthy and positive, basically society-oriented.

By plunging down into your innermost self in silence you make contact with God as healer. As long as you live superficially—noisy and fragmented—in a world of ever-increasing multiplicity and meaninglessness, you will not know the health of body, soul and spirit that God wishes you to enjoy.

Inner health comes through the silencing of your own impulses toward fragmentation. Like Mary, the Mother of God, who opened herself in the annunciation so totally to the Holy Spirit (as St. Luke records in his gospel), you too must allow that word of God to be born within the depths of your being. Your "heart," the core of your being, becomes a womb that in silence and darkness receives God's word. The heavenly Father brings forth his word within you, ever so gently, ever so gradually.

Prayer is listening; it is yielding to the word of God that is being spoken constantly by the indwelling Father through his Holy Spirit. And silence is the language of this communication. Another word for this inner silence is "recollection." It means to be pulled together from your habitual fragmentation to reach a "still point" of attentiveness in order that God might speak to you.

Persons of deep prayer learn to live in this silent recollection, focused upon God as the center of their being. You too can learn to descend to the innermost ground of your being by letting go, by conquering the noise of your own state of limited consciousness whereby you control your life, and letting God become the guide of your life. Through levels of consciousness you sink into the "cloud of unknowing," that state of surrender to God within which the untapped regions beneath the habitual surface of your existence are turned over to God's healing love and control. An important feature of your retreat should be to reach this state of interior silence and recollection. You will thus be gifted by God's Spirit with a kind of knowledge of God that ordinary consciousness on a more discursive level of meditation can never provide. The struggling and searching blindly in darkness gives way to a "hearing" in silence, a seeing "with a loving, striving, blindly beholding the naked being only of God Himself" *(The Cloud of Unknowing)*.

Silence—The Language of Prayer   Silence is the language of deeper, infused prayer that the Holy Spirit gives to God's poor children who hunger and thirst for his word. Ultimately it is the ability to live in mystery. For those who enter into this mystery, there is real communication, deep love, full healing and maturity. But how few are ready to pay the price to enter deeply into mystery and stay there! Prayer is a mystery; silence is its language. To enter into a successful retreat in order to surrender each moment to God's holy will, you need at each moment to want to live in the atmosphere of inner silence which is the same as poverty of spirit or true humility.

Meditation
    1. 1 K 19:9-13: God spoke to Elijah in a still, silent voice.

2. Christ summons you to come aside a while and be quiet, to listen to the word of God. He was silent in prayer on the mountain top. He called his disciples aside to hear his word.

3. Listening: Ps 39; Is 48:12-19; 1 S 3:1-10; Mt 13:10-17; Rv 3:19-22.

FIRST DAY

Alone with the Father

The bible begins with the words: "In the beginning God . . ." (Gn 1:1). God is the beginning of all reality. Before you were created, God existed. Before any creature comes into being, God exists as the source of the being he wishes to share. Making a retreat is similar to gazing at a diamond. God is that diamond of exquisite beauty. You cannot exhaust his simple beauty nor the multiplied perfections he projects into all of creation.

Each meditative consideration in your retreat is a call from the Holy Spirit to take a different *stance* before God. Each vantage point yields some new insight into God's perfection. As the ray of sun is refracted through one part of a beautifully cut diamond and exquisite colors flash in gorgeous array, so each day you will want to view God from different points revealed in his holy word of scripture.

I: Invaded by God

There is a most beautiful phrase that Jesus speaks in St. John's gospel about the central truth of our life. It explains our beginning and our end and all that goes on in our lives in between. Jesus said: "The Father himself loves you" (Jn 16:27). This is the unique revelation that Jesus came to give us. This is what makes Christianity unique among all religions.

ALONE WITH THE ALONE

You are beautiful and unique because God loves you! He truly calls you by your special name (Is 43:1). He even carves your name on the palms of his hands! (Is 49:16). This almighty God tenderly loves you with an everlasting love (Jr 31:3). "I was like someone who lifts an infant close against his cheek; stooping down to him I gave him his food" (Ho 11:4).

But this wonderful and loving God is not removed from us. Our God does not live up above in heaven and drop down upon us the things we need if we pray to him properly. His essence is love, and true love is not only eager to share gifts or to communicate with words or ideas. The essence of love is to gift another with the presence of one's self. Its goal is *communion*, a union of two persons who become one, while each person discovers his or her own uniqueness in being loved by the other.

Infinite Zero   Ponder prayerfully today the awesome mystery of God as love. Before God moves out in loving relationships, even within the Trinity as an *I-Thou* in a *We* community, it is possible to conceive of what the Greek Fathers knew as the *Godhead*. This is, in the words of the 14th-century Rhenish mystic, Meister Eckhart, the "unnatured nature" of God. Mystics referred to this absolutely unknowable God, prior to a loving movement of Person to Person, as the Abyss, the Desert, the Wilderness, the Absolute beyond any being. This is motionless unity and balanced stillness. It is the fullness of being that has not yet spilled out in loving gift.

This is Infinite Zero, for out of this infinite potentiality all other beings emanate and have their being. The concept is in no way negative. Rather, it symbolizes the fullness which embraces all being and hence cannot even be given the name of being.

God's Family   When the spark of love shoots through the darkened void, it sets up a movement of desire. The dark side of God's no-thingness bursts into light as God wishes to know himself in another. The void wishes to come forth and express itself in love. The Father wishes to know and love himself in his Son. He wishes to express and communicate himself by a word, a word that would give full expression to that infinite mind and thrill that mind in ecstatic union as Father and Son in love, the Spirit.

The key word that best expresses God's trinitarian relationships between Father and Son in the Spirit is the Greek word that St. Paul used to express the *emptying* love of Jesus Christ, the image of the Father, on the cross: *kenosis.*

His state was divine,
yet he did not cling
to his equality with God
but emptied himself
to assume the condition of a slave,
and became as men are;
and being as all men are,
he was humbler yet,
even to accepting death,
death on a cross (Ph 2:6-8).

The Father pours out himself in his Spirit of love totally into his Son. As the Son receives this perfect gift and thrills at becoming the Son of so beautiful a Father, he says his eternal "yes" back to the Father in the same Spirit of love. The three persons in ecstasy of union find perfect repose.

Yet repose within the Trinity is never static idleness. Love within the heart of the Trinity is a motionless movement outward to share this realized unity with others. The love of God in three Persons, bursting forth from within to pour itself outwardly into millions and millions of creatures, is the source of all creation. That, which we discover of God's self-giving as Father, Son and Holy Spirit within the

Trinity through revelation, is the basis of the same trinitarian activity throughout our material world.

St. Irenaeus of the second century wrote that God the Father comes to us by his two hands, the Son and the Spirit. God, in the trinitarian relationships of Father, Son and Spirit, gives himself to us and the rest of the created world. These related actions the Greek Fathers were fond of calling the "uncreated energies of love." This is primal grace, namely, God gifts us with himself. The good news that Jesus reveals to us is that God so loves us as to give himself to us.

It is true that God gives us many gifts that are not himself. Yet God's supreme gift in all of his energies of love is to give himself to us so that we can share his very own life. The trinitarian presence is inside every atom of nature, working at all times to reach the point where we will be able to receive him as Father, Son and Spirit in communion:

"And eternal life is this:
to know you,
the only true God,
and Jesus Christ whom you have sent" (Jn 17:3).

Grace   Grace is primarily uncreated since it is the triune Persons gifting us with divine life which is none other than union with the Trinity. In such a vision of Christian faith as seen from God's immanent, loving presence in all created things, there is no "nature" that is purely nature without also being permeated with the sacred, the divine, the living and actively loving presence of God, Father, Son and Spirit.

We are "graced" at all times by God in his energies of love. These divine energies always surround us and lovingly call us to respond to God's word living within us and discovered in the context of the events of our daily living. As we cooperate with God's grace as his divine uncreated energies unveil each moment of our daily life, we enter into the process of *theosis* or divinization. This is to become totally integrated and fulfilled in our body-soul-spirit relationships with God, with people and with the entire material cosmos.

Children of God   We are made participators in God's divine nature (2 P 1:4). This is the great dignity to which we have been called, to be really children of God.

Think of the love that the Father has lavished on us,
by letting us be called God's children;
and that is what we are (1 Jn 3:1).

The spirit you received is not the spirit of slaves bringing fear into your lives again; it is the spirit of sons, and it makes us cry out, "Abba, Father!" The Spirit himself and our spirit bear united witness that we are children of God. And if we are children we are heirs as well: heirs of God and coheirs with Christ, sharing his sufferings so as to share his glory (Rm 8:15-17).

The purpose of our life is to contemplate God everywhere, for that is where he is. Discover him as Father, Son and Holy Spirit, ". . . since it is in him that we live, and move, and exist . . ." (Ac 17:28). This Trinity abides in us (Jn 14:23) and yet surrounds, permeates, invades and bombards us from all sides, within all creatures that we encounter.

Finding God in all things as he loves us with the gift of his love, we are to respond to that transforming love by living in self-sacrificing love for God. We will want every thought, word and deed to be saturated with our love in return for God's love. We should desire to praise and glorify the triune God by our life.

Before the world was made, he chose us, chose us in Christ,
to be holy and spotless, and to live through love in his
presence,
determining that we should become his adopted sons,
through Jesus Christ
for his own kind purposes,

31

to make us praise the glory of his grace,
his free gift to us in the Beloved,
in whom, through his blood, we gain our freedom, the
    forgiveness
of our sins (Ep 1:4-7).

Meditation
    Prayerfully ponder:
Psalm 139 — God knows us in every detail.

II: *The Humility of God*

If God is love (1 Jn 4:8,16), he is also humble. His
humility is seen both in his utter freedom first to love us and
then in his mysterious desire to wait for our love in return.
The God we can understand is he who gives us a share in his
goodness. The God we cannot understand or even ap-
preciate is he who waits lovingly for us with an attitude not
only of wanting our love but also, apparently, of needing our
love.

God's Free Love   Have you ever loved another person
greatly? The more you gave of yourself to that person, the
more you experienced true freedom. You knew that no one,
not even the loved one, was forcing your love, yet you *freely*
loved that person. Did you love then because you were free,
or did you become free by loving?

With God love and freedom cannot be separated. There
can be no outside force urging God to love. There can be in
God no intrinsic compulsion for him to love us as though he
who is perfect still needs to attain some perfection by loving.
Within the Trinity God is love and God is free. That same
free love God pours out toward us.

Every page of the Old Testament teaches us that God
freely wants to share his divine life with us. In Hebrew the

word *aheb* expresses God's free, unconditional love. It is not because of what Israel is that God gives his love to his chosen people:

> If Yahweh set his heart on you and chose you, it was not because you outnumbered other peoples: you were the least of all peoples. It was for love of you . . . that Yahweh brought you out with his mighty hand and redeemed you from the house of slavery, from the power of Pharaoh king of Egypt. Know then that Yahweh, your God, is God indeed, the faithful God who is true to his covenant and his graciousness for a thousand generations . . . (Dt 7:7-10).

God is completely free in his love to choose whom he will love. The beautiful Hebrew word *hesed* describes God's act of loving, condescending kindness in choosing Israel and pledging his fidelity *(emet)* to use his power and mercy to stand by his covenanted people.

> I will betroth you to myself forever,
> betroth you with integrity and justice,
> with tenderness and love;
> I will betroth you to myself with faithfulness,
> and you will come to know Yahweh (Ho 2:19-20).

Jesus, the New Covenant   God's love for us reached its fullest when he gave us his only-begotten Son.

> God's love for us was revealed
> when God sent into the world his only Son
> so that we could have life through him;
> this is the love I mean:
> not our love for God,
> but God's love for us when he sent his Son
> to be the sacrifice that takes our sins away (1 Jn 4:9-10).

The Word of God pitched his tent of meeting among us. Now God pledges to speak perfectly to us through this man, Jesus Christ. If we obey his commandments, we obey the Father and we will have eternal life (Jn 14:21,23).

ALONE WITH THE ALONE

The gift of Jesus is God's gift of the entire trinitarian family, for, as we receive Jesus, the risen Lord, and surrender in loving obedience to his lordship, we receive the Father and his Spirit. The Spirit of Jesus risen convinces us of the staggering truth that by Jesus we have been made into the people of God:

> But you are a chosen race, a royal priesthood, a consecrated nation, a people set apart to sing the praises of God who called you out of the darkness into his wonderful light. Once you were not a people at all and now you are the People of God; once you were outside the mercy and now you have been given mercy (1 P 2:9-10).

Darkness in God   In retreat after retreat you could thrill to God's great outpoured love for you, especially in Jesus Christ. But in this retreat may God reveal to you the other side of his great love. May you discover his awesome humility that waits for the gift of yourself. May he even show you that he needs your love to fill up the love of his Son Jesus as his eternal response of "yes" to the Father.

This is a mystery that cannot be argued by human concepts. You can only intuit the mystery of God's desire for your returned love in humble prayer as you call upon the Holy Spirit to enlighten you. The Spirit reveals to you in your own human love relationships that love in you or in God can never be only in one direction. Love goes out and gives to another the gift of the lover. We might call that the *animus* of the initiator.

God first loves us. This is symbolized in holy scripture as God, pure light, without any imperfection, going out of himself in gift to us (1 Jn 1:5-7). God is always giving himself to us, directly through Jesus Christ and his Spirit, and indirectly through the created world.

The Anima in God   But love is circular. It goes forth in self-gift, and it also waits in aweful expectancy to receive the return of love in the gift of the other. In the past we have placed the accent on God's perfection and completeness, even in the case of human beings who do not return his love. But in maintaining his immutability and perfection we sometimes fail to see that God really wants our love. We cannot comprehend how God could really want our love. More, we think it heresy to believe that we can make God happy by our returned love.

Scripture shows us God meeting human beings in darkness. This should not be conceived of as an imperfection in God. On the contrary, this is part of his perfection as Father that he really does want our love as a sharing in the total love of his Son.

Darkness is the scriptural image of God as *toward us,* yet also of God as vulnerable and capable of being rejected by his people. "Cloud and Darkness surround him" (Ps 97:2). Yahweh was in a pillar of cloud guiding his people by day in the desert (Ex 13:21). It was in the darkness of the cloud on top of Mount Sinai that God spoke to Moses (Ex 24:16-17). Thus darkness is the symbol used in scripture to describe God in his humble condescension to communicate his love to us and to invite us unto communion with him as we respond.

The Darkness in Jesus   From the Old Testament God pursues his people in love. But he also is humble and waiting, vulnerable to his people's fickleness when they turn away and reject his offered love.

This is the side of God the Father that Jesus revealed to us in the New Testament. Jesus shows us in his own earthly life, an image of the Father's life, how vulnerable and open he is to receive the love of human beings. He suffers their coldness and indifference. He weeps over Jerusalem as a symbol of the whole world. Like a hen he would wish to gather all human beings as chicks under his motherly wings, but we so often would not consent (Lk 13:34-35).

But the greatest manifestation of God the Father's waiting vulnerability is shown in the symbol of the darkness that shrouded Jesus on the cross. There he is broken and rejected, by his disciples, his Jewish people; seemingly even abandoned by his heavenly Father.

Can you believe that God the Father remains immutable and unconcerned as he sees Jesus, his beloved Son, suffer and die amid such darkness? Is it too far-fetched to believe that Jesus images the Father's readiness to suffer in him as he with Jesus waits for our loving response? The power of God is in his weakness and humility to be ready to endure everything in the dark emptiness of Jesus in order to receive our love.

In Jesus' darkness God flashes forth on the cross as a flaming meteor of love. "For me Jesus dies," we can whisper; thus God shows us the extent of his readiness to suffer and be rejected in order to wait for us to turn back to him. "As the Father has loved me, so I have loved you" (Jn 15:9). We have no way of knowing the love and the waiting darkness in God our Father except through the imaged suffering love of Jesus for us.

Filling Up the Body of Christ   The Father pours the fullness of his being into Jesus Christ. "In his body, lives the fullness of divinity, and in him you too find your own fulfillment, in the one who is the head of every Sovereignty and Power" (Col 2:9-10). The Father waits eagerly to be called out of darkness into the realized light of being well-pleased by the total Christ — Jesus risen as the head, and we human beings as his body.

> Now the Church is his body,
> he is its head.
> As he is the Beginning,

he was first to be born from the dead,
so that he should be first in every way;
because God wanted all perfection
to be found in him
and all things to be reconciled through him and for him,
everything in heaven and everything on earth,
when he made peace
by his death on the cross (Col 1:18-20).

We see now that God created us to be a vital part of his only Son, Jesus Christ. The Father within the Trinity truly wants and needs the response of his Son in total self-surrendering love, in order that he may be called out of the darkness of potentially being loved by his Son to the actuality of the light of being Father in realized love received from his Son.

On the cross Jesus passed over from darkness to light, from death to glory, and now the Father was loved in a new manner, not only by his divine Son, but by that Son as totally human. The Father is well-pleased in this love. Something new has been given to him for which he waited eagerly all the earthly life of Jesus.

You and I belong to Christ by living our baptism. He is the head and we are his members. The heavenly Father eagerly desires to be recognized and loved as the one Father of the total Jesus Christ, head and members. This is another way of looking at the end of our human existence: to grow daily by dying to our selfish isolation and rising in self-forgetting love to a new oneness in the risen Lord; and thus to call God our Father, the same Father of Jesus and of us since he has come from darkness into the light of a new relationship with his Son. The Father loves in his Spirit only one Person, his only-begotten Son.

But your dignity is that by God's election and grace you are one with Christ, one body, one faith, one Spirit with one Father over all (Ep 4:4-6). The Father truly loves you and needs your love as he needs the full Christ to call him the fully realized Father of us all.

Meditation
    Pray over:
Isaiah 43; 49: 15-16 — God has called us by name.

III: *Our Loving Father*

The purpose of our lives on earth is to live in the presence of God as Father in oneness with Jesus Christ who releases from within us his Spirit of love who enables us to adore the all-holy God by seeking in loving obedience to do all for his glory. This was why Jesus Christ, the Word, was made flesh. He came among us to reveal to us his tender, loving Father as being truly involved and caring for us in all details of our lives.

How long it takes all of us to reach this key point of Christian revelation so as to experience habitually by deep faith, hope and love that our Father loves us in each event of our lives! Are we even now at the present stage of our spiritual life able to believe and act upon this truth phrased by St. Paul: "We know that by turning everything to their good God co-operates with all those who love him, with all those that he has called according to his purpose" (Rm 8:28)?

Perhaps one reason why it takes many years of adult living before we can have a deep devotion to our heavenly Father is that we need to purify and correct the experiences of fatherhood that we received from our earthly father. No matter how good a father he was to us, he still was limited and left us with something less than an image of a perfect father.

There is a more important reason, however, for our delayed devotion to God-Father. We need many years of living on this earth before we fall in love and can reach a state of receiving love from another and returning that love with true self-sacrifice. As we stop using other persons for our own needs and live out of loving service to the ones we love, we can move away from using our heavenly Father to satisfy all our earthly needs and move in purity of heart to a love similar to that which Jesus showed his Father.

A Redemptive Revelation   Jesus' redemptive work can be seen as the work of revealing the Father to us. Through his released Spirit he makes it possible for us to become truly brothers and sisters with him and with every other human being. Jesus, through his Spirit, makes it possible for us to continuously experience the Father's infinite, personalized love for us by experiencing his own love, an image of the Father's love.

The Incarnate Word abides in us and releases within us his Spirit who reveals at each moment of our lives the tender, powerful love of the Father for us individually. In prayer and in living the sacrament of the present moment we are to grow daily under the power of the Holy Spirit in the loving knowledge that we have a heavenly Father who loves and cares for us. This requires an inner silence in which we listen to the Father love us into a greater oneness with his Son through his Spirit. Prayer becomes this continual communion with God-Father as the source of our being. Such attentive listening flows from our own inner poverty and brokenness as we continually cry out, "Abba, Father!"

Your Father in Scripture   We do not have to imagine what our Father is like. We turn to holy scripture and Jesus to discover his Father to be our Father, too. Turn to Psalm 139 to discover God as an involved, energetic God, close to you at all times, fashioning you and knowing all your thoughts:

ALONE WITH THE ALONE

Yahweh, you examine me and know me,
you know if I am standing or sitting,
you read my thoughts from far away,
whether I walk or lie down, you are watching,
you know every detail of my conduct. . . .

Where could I go to escape your spirit?
Where could I flee from your presence?
If I climb the heavens, you are there,
there too, if I lie in Sheol.
If I flew to the point of sunrise,
or westward across the sea,
your hand would still be guiding me,
your right hand holding me. . . .

It was you who created my inmost self,
and put me together in my mother's womb;
for all these mysteries I thank you:
for the wonder of myself, for the wonder of your works. . . .

God, examine me and know my heart,
probe me and know my thoughts;
make sure I do not follow pernicious ways,
and guide me in the way that is everlasting (Ps 139:1-3; 7-10;
13-14; 23-24).

This Creator-God is not merely omnipotent; he is also a
tender, loving Father who encourages us to trust in his
goodness at all times. What beautiful images we find in the
Old Testament of a Father who stoops down and lovingly
embraces his people! "How Yahweh carried you, as a man
carries his child, all along the road you travelled on the way
to this place" (Dt 1:31).

You can walk through rivers and you will not drown.
Fires will surround you, yet you will not be burned because
Yahweh will protect you. You are not to fear since God is
with you always (Is 43:1-3,5). With Job you, too, can ask:

"But surely he sees how I behave, does he not count all my steps?" (Jb 31:4).

No more tender picture of God's love can be found than that described by the Prophet Isaiah:

> Does a woman forget her baby at the breast
> or fail to cherish the son of her womb?
> Yet even if these forget,
> I will never forget you (Is 49:15).

The Father of the New Testament   Jesus came, not to destroy the Old Testament revelation, but to fulfill it. He not only teaches in so many ways about our heavenly Father, but he brings it about through his Spirit that we can experience this eternal, almighty Father as living intimately within us as we live as one with Jesus.

Jesus assures you, as one who came from the Father and speaks to you the truth about him, that you must no longer fear or be overly anxious about temporal things. Your Father knows all your needs and he loves you. Therefore, he will answer all your needs if you put him first in your life. Prayerfully consider Luke 12:22-34 or Matthew 6:25-33:

> Now if that is how God clothes the grass in the field which is there today and thrown into the furnace tomorrow, how much more will he look after you, you men of little faith! But you, you must not set your hearts on things to eat and things to drink; nor must you worry. It is the pagans of this world who set their hearts on all these things. Your Father well knows you need them. No; set your hearts on his kingdom, and these other things will be given you as well. There is no need to be afraid, little flock, for it has pleased your Father to give you the kingdom (Lk 12:28-32).

You will know when you accept the love of the Father, for then there will be no fear.

> In love there can be no fear,
> but fear is driven out by perfect love (1 Jn 4:18).

Abandonment of Jesus to His Father   Jesus at all times during his earthly life experienced the loving presence of his Father. This consuming love, poured into his heart at each moment by God's Spirit, gave him his sense of identity and unique personhood: "The world will realize that it was you who sent me and that I have loved them as much as you loved me" (Jn 17:23).

Nothing could separate Jesus from the Father, for they both were one (Jn 17:21-23). The Father rejoices in Jesus who always pleased the Father. Covered by the Father's burning love for his Son, Jesus sought at every moment to surrender himself to the Father from whom he received everything as a loving gift.

Jesus Most Human   Jesus saw the Father working in all the events of his life (Jn 5:17) and he rejoiced to work with him. In all of his human experiences — experiencing a beautiful sunset over Lake Tiberias, a good meal, the touch of a loved one, the rejection of a friend, even suffering and death — Jesus saw the smiling face of his loving Father. He abandoned himself to that inside presence of the Father by surrendering only to him to please him.

What freedom to be fully human Jesus enjoyed as he met the Father's love in all the beautiful as well as the broken situations of his human life! He could afford to be totally human and totally alive because he was serenely at one in peace and joy with the Father. He did not ignore the human situation, but he soared higher to find the Father calling him at each moment and in each event to become the Son of the Father by his perfect surrendering obedience: "Yes, Father. Whatever you wish, may that be done!"

Your Abandonment to the Father   You cannot surrender to an unknown person. But to the degree that you have experienced the Father's infinite love for you as imaged by Jesus always dying for you, to that same degree you will desire, not as a law or duty, but as your greatest privilege, to surrender to please the Father.

This is impossible under your own power, but it is possible by the love of God that is poured into your heart by the Spirit of Jesus (Rm 5:5). The essence of loving abandonment to your heavenly Father is a twofold movement. It is a movement away from your self-centeredness. It is also a positive movement toward God as you are enlightened by God's grace in each moment to intuit the will of God. Love of God is what brought you into being, and love as your response to God's love is the goal of your life.

Such loving abandonment extends to past, present and future events. But the only point of meeting God in loving surrender is the sacrament of the present moment. Abandonment to God's good pleasure in the event of this moment means that you trust in God's faithfulness to provide for all your needs. But it also means that you use your talents to cooperate with God's designs. God may give you health, but you must exercise, eat and sleep properly and avoid being overly anxious. Perhaps at times you will have to take medicine or have an operation. Being meek and gentle may mean being strong and firm in disciplining your children or those whom you teach. God will provide for all your needs, but you may have to look long and hard for employment or work diligently even in monotony.

The End of Your Life   You have prayerfully pondered today the purpose that the triune God has in creating you. You see that you are, in the words of St. Irenaeus, an empty receptacle to be filled by God's gifts. Father, Son and Spirit pour out their personalized love for you in all of their uncreated energies of love. The Trinity wishes to communicate to you its family of one and many, an *I-Thou* in a *We* community, in order to lead you to a loving surrender in communion or oneness within that trinitarian family.

The goal of your life, which in this time and that to come is an ever-continuing process of realization, is to surrender yourself in love to God. Such surrender in order to please God means a constant death or detachment from your own desires as the ultimate concern in your life.

By dying to yourself you are to rise to a new level of consciousness of being one with Jesus Christ according to whose image and likeness you have been created (Gn 1:26). Putting on the mind of Christ Jesus, you are to live only to please the Father in all things. Thus you daily grow into the freedom of a child of God. You freely give your life to God as gift only to receive it back in a quickening of new identity that allows you to give yourself as God does and, with God living within you, to love all who come into your life.

You have been made out of love. You become your true self only by loving God and neighbor as Jesus does, and with Jesus loving God the Father and all creatures within you. The prayer of Charles de Foucauld on abandonment well summarizes the goal of your life:

> Father, I abandon myself into your hands. Do with me what you will. And for whatever you may do, I thank you. I am ready for all. I accept all. Let only your will be done in me and in all your creatures. I wish no more than this, O Lord. Into your hands I commend my life. I offer it to you with all the love of my heart. For I love you, God, and so need to give myself, to surrender myself into your hands without reserve, and with boundless confidence, for you are my Father.

Meditation
    Consider prayerfully:
Luke 12:21-31 — We are not to worry about our life.

My Dark Side

We have moved around this beautiful diamond, God. We saw his beauty shine through varying views of fluffy clouds in the sunny sky, of babbling mountain streams, of birds creating symphonies of song in the early morning, of the spangling reds and pinks and oranges of brilliant sunsets over the ocean. We looked up into his smiling countenance and joyfully whispered with Jesus, "Our Father!"

But today we view God from a totally different vantage point: our brokenness. We want as the fruit of this day the courage to enter into the dark areas of our life. We want to know, with St. Paul, that there is sin in our members (Rm 7:23). We want to experience sin as a cancer that shoots through our whole being, in all our relationships. We want to see sin also as our oneness with the brokenness of the whole world that groans in travail (Rm 8:22).

We beg also for the great grace to realize in our brokenness that Jesus is the incarnate, healing mercy of God. As we fear our locked-in enslavement and inability to set ourselves free, we cry out for hope in Jesus' healing love. We can be healed by God's mercy! Come, Lord Jesus! *Marana tha.*

I: My Brokenness

It was once so easy for us to handle the subject of sin. In preparing for confession or during past retreats, we placed ourselves before the laws given by God through his church: How many times did I violate this or that law? When all our sinfulness was carefully tabulated according to "species and numbers," we went before the priest as penitent criminals before a judge. It was a relief to unburden the guilt from taboos violated. We went from the confessional relieved, but hardly aware of what sin was all about and, above all, oblivious of the depths of inner brokenness within us that should have been crying out for healing.

Brokenness   It should be relatively easy for us to recognize the increasing brokenness that appears as we grow older. Each day we feel heaviness in the body, dragging us unwilling to our final day. But it takes much courage and silence to enter into hidden areas of our being and to encounter there the mountains and mountains of psychic and spiritual brokenness.

Under these mountains that have been pushed into the darkness of the unconscious are smouldering volcanoes of seething past hurts. What fears rise up like specters out of the mist and fog of our past! What raw experiences trigger anger, hatred, unforgiveness! What moods of depression, melancholy and loneliness come over us when we reflect on the wasted parts of our life!

Then deeper still we go to stand before God in our spiritual brokenness. We see what sinful tendencies lie within us, what heinous evil acts we are capable of committing. We see the strangle hold of past habits exercising their enslavement over us. God lets a soft light of what could have been shine into our darkness as we see the many areas of omissions, of good deeds not done, of God's gentle whispers unheeded.

Sin   Sin, we begin to see, is more than a violation of a law. In the Byzantine liturgy, before receiving the Eucharist both priest and people pray together for forgiveness of all sin, deliberate and inherited. Sin is anything that prevents God from being God in our life. It is as much the brokenness of our ancestors that we have inherited as our own willfulness. It is the "sin of the world" or a sharing in original sin.

We open ourselves to the cancerous, cosmic influences of sin by being born into this world. And to this inherited evil we add our own deliberate sin. Our whole being shudders at the fragmentation. We feel caught in a prison of darkness and yet we see a delicate ray of light leading us out through the crack of *metanoia,* a conversion to the Lord.

A voice, ever so softly, whispers in our hearts the hopeful words of the prophet Joel:

> Come back to me with all your heart,
> fasting, weeping, mourning.
> Let your hearts be broken, not your garments torn,
> turn to Yahweh your God again,
> for he is all tenderness and compassion,
> slow to anger, rich in graciousness,
> and ready to relent (Jl 2:12-13).

On this day we want to enter into a state of bereavement. We close the curtains over our windows and in darkness we prostrate ourselves on the floor before our God. We seek with God's grace to experience the split within us of light and darkness, of union with God and alienation from him: Why do I do what I know I should not do? Who can deliver me from such bondage?

> But I am unspiritual; I have been sold as a slave to sin. I cannot understand my own behavior. I fail to carry out the things I want to do, and I find myself doing the very things I hate. When I act against my own will, that means I have a self that acknowledges that the Law is good, and so the thing behaving in that way is not my self but sin living in me. The fact is, I know of nothing good living in me — living, that is,

47

in my unspiritual self—for though the will to do what is good is in me, the performance is not, with the result that instead of doing the good things I want to do, I carry out the sinful things I do not want. When I act against my will, then, it is not my true self doing it, but sin which lives in me. . . . This is what makes me a prisoner of that law of sin which lives inside my body. What a wretched man I am! Who will rescue me from this body doomed to death? Thanks be to God through Jesus Christ our Lord! (Rm 7:14-24).

The Gift of Tears   A prostitute once knelt before Jesus as he sat at table with Simon, the Pharisee. She washed his feet with her tears of repentance and wiped them with her hair and anointed them with ointment. Jesus says she must have been forgiven her many sins because she loved much (Lk 7:36-50). Perhaps today we, too, can be given great faith in God's loving mercy so that we can experience his forgiveness and be healed of all brokenness. We desire to weep tears of sorrow and repentance at experiencing how much God loves us in spite of our own ingratitude and indifference.

The Fathers of the desert in the early centuries of Christianity sat day and night begging for God's mercy which they felt was given them by God when they wept tears of compunction. Seeing the depths of brokenness within themselves and the evil they shared with a broken world, they cried out the Jesus Prayer: "Lord, Jesus Christ, Son of God, have mercy on me, a sinner!"

Such tears can have a powerful action in uprooting and destroying our sins and brokenness and all the elements that enslave us in our false selves. If we live superficially and never penetrate beyond the surface of our being, we will not see the urgency for crying out to Jesus, the Divine Physician, for deep healing. We beg today for true self-knowledge of our sinfulness. Above all, we wish to stretch out in hope toward the Trinity that dwells within us. Turning within to face our inner darkness, we let the light of God's tender mercy and love burst upon us.

Meditation
   Prayerful considerations:
1. Psalm 51 — David's repentance.
2. Luke 7:36-50 — The tears of a prostitute.
3. Joel 2:12-13 — Turn to Yahweh with fasting and weeping.
4. Romans 7:14-24 — Sin in my members.
5. Luke 15:11-32 — Parable of the Prodigal Son.

II: *Lord, Jesus Christ, Have Mercy on Me, a Sinner*

You have dared with God's grace to look honestly at the broken condition in which you find yourself. There are two movements in a conversion toward a more complete surrender to God. The first movement you have reckoned with in the previous considerations. You have been led into the arid desert of your heart. There the Holy Spirit showed you, as Ezekiel saw (Ez 37:1-14), the dried bones of your past and present. You shuddered in fearful amazement at the depths of sterility and darkness that you honestly claimed to be due to "sin in your members."

Now pray to the Holy Spirit that you may open yourself in prayerful consideration to the second movement of a conversion to your heavenly Father. This consists in wanting to get rid of the "husks of swine" (Lk 15:16), to rise and go back to your Father's home. It is a burning prayer honestly poured out from your heart that by God's mercy you can start over. You can be that noble and beautiful child of so loving a Father. You can become, by his power, your true self.

Let this meditation be a contemplative stretching-out toward Jesus Christ. He is the love and mercy that images the Father's love for you. God so loved you in your broken-ness that he sent his only-begotten Son into that sinful world of yours so that you may believe in him and have eternal life (Jn 3:16).

Without Jesus there would be no hope for you in your brokenness. It is not enough to claim your sinfulness as honestly and sincerely as you can. You need to hope in God's infinite mercy that he can condescend to you and pick you up. Pray to experience how Yahweh in the person of Jesus Christ is waiting to enfold you in his loving arms. "I was like someone who lifts an infant close against his cheek; stooping down to him I gave him his food" (Ho 11:4).

There is hope for you in Christ Jesus. He is the pledge of your salvation. He alone can save you from your sinful condition, heal you and bring you eternal life, a share in his own divine life inherited from the Father.

Fear of God   A most important element in our return to God through Jesus Christ is a wholesome religious fear. We stretch out to Jesus Christ but in body, soul and spirit we realize that he is not merely a good and loving man, but that he is totally God. He is Lord! He rules the universe! He is the Son of God from all eternity, the Divine Word in whom all things in the heavens and on earth have their being (Col 1:16; Jn 1:2). Such fear for Christ is an awe-filled meeting with him in his supreme transcendence.

Rudolf Otto, in his book, *The Idea of the Holy,* argues that the experience of God is qualitatively unique and describes it variously as experience of the "numinous," the "holy," the "other." Such an experience brings one forcibly in contact with something (Someone) so separate, so great, so powerful, that one is, at least initially, unable to assimilate the experience in ordinary ways. One experiences the "other," first as *mysterium tremendum,* and the experience is one full of a specifically religious dread. The dread results from an awareness of the object of the experience as something totally other, incomprehensible and powerful.

This awareness manifests itself in a sense of our ontological worthlessness, the sinful creatureliness upon which we have been meditating. Although the experience is dreadful, the religious object is fascinating. So rather than the simple avoidance which usually accompanies a fear of something, we are inevitably drawn into acquaintance with the "other." This acquaintance is not on an intellectual level. The "other" is ineffable, supremely mysterious, until it chooses to reveal more of itself.

Jesus Christ is Lord, Son of God, the image of the invisible God that no human being can ever look upon and live (Ex 33:21). And yet this trembling before his majesty, much as St. Peter did when Jesus filled the nets of the fishermen with fish (Lk 5:8-9), not only induces an awesome fear ("Depart from me, for I am a sinful man, O Lord"), but it creates a fascination *(mysterium fascinans)* and a burning desire to hold on to Jesus as did St. Peter who left everything and followed him.

This fear of God is found often on the pages of the Old Testament. It is a rich and complex concept that is different from our ordinary experience of being afraid. Psalm 33 best describes this fear that is mingled with hope:

> But see how the eye of Yahweh is on those who fear him,
> on those who rely on his love,
> to rescue their souls from death
> and keep them alive in famine (Ps 33:18-19).

The prophet Daniel tells that he was so overcome by awareness of his worthlessness that he trembled, even to the point of fainting. And yet, he was fascinated and showed a humble willingness to offer himself, even though he realized how unworthy he was, to the "other" (Dn 10).

Fear of God in the New Testament   Even in the gospel of God's love we find over and over again this important emphasis on fear of God. We recognize it in the response of Zechariah to the angel — he was afraid, and others were aware from his appearance that he had encountered something holy (Lk 1:12). Mary, the Mother of Jesus, had a similar experience, so that the angel Gabriel hastened to reassure her (Lk 1:29). As the angels hailed the birth of Christ, the shepherds were terrified (Lk 2:10).

The disciples of Jesus sensed that they were in the presence of someone great and mysterious and are recorded as being afraid on several occasions. After Jesus had calmed the sea, "They were filled with awe and said to one another, 'Who can this be? Even the wind and sea obey him' " (Mk 4:41). Similarly at the transfiguration, they were frightened and filled with awe (Mk 9:6).

Not only the disciples, but all those who witnessed the miracles of Jesus were aware of the presence of the "numinous," and responded with fear and awe. After Jesus had raised the widow's son, "Fear seized them all, and they began to praise God. 'A great prophet has arisen among us!' they said; and 'God has visited his people' " (Lk 7:16 — NAB).

St. John Chrysostom captures this sense of awesome fear as he describes the tension of holy dread that makes a person tremble, become numb and unable to grasp or make sense of the encounter, while at the same time being filled with a spirit of joyful adoration. The dual response of fear and adoration is joined by faith since we have witnessed the mystery of God and must render glory to him. The natural and appropriate human response before the face of God is, therefore, threefold: awe, adoration and faith.

The Jesus Prayer   It is little wonder that in the fourth century, when the Holy Spirit again drove certain *anawim,* the poor ones of God, into the desert, those men and women reduced the entire message of the gospel to the prayer called in Eastern tradition the Jesus Prayer: "Lord, Jesus Christ, Son of God, have mercy on me, a sinner!" They knew and experienced more and more, as they pronounced the name of Jesus with awe, adoration and faith, that his name was an extension of his person, gloriously risen and sharing with them his risen life, as he dwelt in them.

The name released the awesome power of the resurrected Lord Jesus to come and bring healing and salvation to them in their brokenness. St. Peter preached: "For of all the names in the world given to men, this is the only one by which we can be saved" (Ac 4:12). St. Paul exhorts the Philippians to call upon the name of Jesus that is above all other names (Ph 2:9-10). Jesus himself in St. John's gospel reveals the power of Jesus' name to intercede for his disciples before his heavenly Father: "Until now you have not asked for anything in my name. . . . Anything you ask for from the Father he will grant in my name" (Jn 16: 23, 24).

You, too, can experience the healing power of the presence of the Lord Jesus by crying out to him unceasingly during your retreat. It is the cry of the blind man on the road to Jericho that now becomes yours: "Jesus, son of David, have pity on me" (Lk 18:38). It is the *Lord, have mercy; Christ have mercy* of the liturgy of each day.

The Transfiguring Lord Jesus   Part of your healing and transformation into Jesus and his risen life comes as you experience him as the Lord of glory and transfiguring power. He possesses "the fullness of him who fills the whole creation" (Ep 1:23). Centering upon his awesome majesty in his glorified risen life, you open up to his transfiguring power to take you from your brokenness and sinfulness and lead you into a new creation (2 Cor 5:17-18). In such contemplative union with the transfiguring power of Jesus, allow his "otherness" as Lord of the universe to pour over you and dispel all that is not Christlike in you.

The risen, transfiguring Lord Jesus leads you into the presence of his released Spirit of love. The Holy Spirit of Jesus fills you, broken and contrite of heart, with a deep knowledge of God's tremendous love and mercy, on the one hand; and on the other, he leads you to a realization of your own poverty, sinfulness and unworthiness even to stand in God's presence. He softens the awesomeness of the Father by shortening the distance across the abyss that separates you from him as he leads you to a constantly new experience of Jesus as the bridge, as the way that leads you into the heart of the Father.

Sensitized by the indwelling Holy Spirit, you can yield yourself completely to the promptings of the Holy Spirit, always speaking to you from within, to comprehend the word of God in holy scripture and in the existential event of each moment. He gives you the ability to live in the tension of the farawayness of God and his most intimate closeness dwelling within you through Jesus Christ. You learn to yield to his illumination and knowledge that far surpasses anything you could reason with your own mind.

Like the early disciples who repented of their sinfulness and betrayal of their Master, you now realize the transfiguring presence of Jesus leading you from your brokenness to a new life. Sorrow mingles with joy as you experience the words of your Master: "Happy those who mourn: they shall be comforted" (Mt 5:5).

Who Sees Me Sees the Father   Above all, the Lord Jesus, seeing your humbled and contrite heart, pours into your heart the love of the Father. You spring into a new realization that you are beautiful in the freshly realized love of the Father's love for you. You thrill, even in your brokenness, to know that with Jesus you have become the Father's child and a coheir of heaven forever (Rm 8:17).

As you repeat the name of Jesus, the presence of Jesus within you through his Spirit generates in your heart a burning love for the Father. Mountains of anxieties dissolve in the sea of God's infinite love as you cast them out in the name of Jesus and in the powerful, fatherly love of his Father and your Father. The Father is pleased as he sees you now aware that Christ, in St. Paul's words, lives in your heart "through faith, and then, planted in love and built on love, you will with all the saints have strength to grasp the breadth and the length, the height and the depth; until, knowing the love of Christ, which is beyond all knowledge, you are filled with the utter fullness of God" (Ep 3:17-19).

The Father begets us as his children when we unite ourselves with Jesus. We become truly his children as we become more and more one with Jesus. The Father in the parable of the Prodigal Son truly rejoices to see that you have returned to him and confessed your sinfulness. Now he covers you with his strong, tender hands of love. He prepares the allegorical banquet for you in which he gives you to eat forever the Lamb of God (Lk 15:23-24).

From sorrow you have been led into joy that no one can take from you. From suffering in your brokenness and crying out in anguish to see the face of God, you experience the risen Jesus releasing within the depths of your heart his Spirit who unveils the face of the heavenly Father to you. The kingdom of heaven has come to you. Your darkness has turned to the light of Christ who shines within you. Your weeping has turned to joy because Jesus Christ, who is Lord and Son of God, truly has shown mercy upon you. And your joy will last forever!

> The throne of God and of the Lamb will be in its place in the city; his servants will worship him, they will see him face to face, and his name will be written on their foreheads. It will

never be night again and they will not need lamplight or sunlight, because the Lord God will be shining on them. They will reign for ever and ever (Rv 22:3-5).

Meditation

1. Pray the Jesus Prayer for a half-hour, synchronizing it with your breathing.

2. For another half-hour, review in the presence of the Blessed Trinity your daily life in the light of your relationships:

a. with the Trinity—Father, Son and Holy Spirit;

b. with your neighbors, especially those you live with most intimately in "stable monotony," in your family or community living;

c. with yourself: body, soul, spirit.

III: *Healing Love*

No one living on earth is without some *brokenness.* You have meditated on your own brokenness honestly before a loving God. So much of what you discovered as impediments came into your life and fashioned your character, not only from your acts of deliberately turning away from God, but from the actions of so many other persons upon your life.

A world that groans in travail (Rm 8:23) and surrounds you with its filth, sordidness and corruption continuously exerts upon you an evil force sucking you into its mire. A church that is the virgin-spouse of Jesus Christ has had its negative influence upon you through its sinful and worldly members. You sense your powerlessness to stretch out to Jesus Christ and leave the confining prison of brokenness.

Is there an answer to so much evil, brokenness and suffering in your life? Is there someone who can say to you as a certain healer long ago said to a paralytic, "Get up, and pick up your bed and go off home" (Mt 9:6)? Out of the depths of your fears, guilt, doubts, frustrations, anger, loneliness and depression, you cry out to the Lord with the Psalmist:

> From the depths I call to you, Yahweh,
> Lord, listen to my cry for help
> Listen compassionately
>   to my pleading!
>
> If you never overlooked our sins, Yahweh,
> Lord, could anyone survive?
> But you do forgive us:
>   and for that we revere you.
>
> I wait for Yahweh, my soul waits for him,
>   I rely on his promise,
>   my soul relies on the Lord
>   more than a watchman on the coming of dawn.
>
> Let Israel rely on Yahweh
>   as much as the watchman on the dawn!
> For it is with Yahweh that mercy is to be found,
> and a generous redemption;
> it is he who redeems Israel
>   from all their sins (Ps 130).

Only God Can Save   Your Christian faith convinces you that God truly wishes to share his eternal life with you by giving you his beloved Son, Jesus Christ (Jn 3:16-17). He is the Divine Physician and he comes as your saviour and healer. He comes to give you life more abundantly (Jn 10:10). As he went about Palestine healing all the broken ones in body, soul and spirit (Mt 4:23-24; 9:35; 10:1), so Jesus still can heal all broken ones, including you, who are now living on earth. Today he will stretch out his healing hands of mercy and love to you, if you only believe.

He asks you today: "Do you believe that I can heal you and that I wish to do so?" He healed and transformed his weak and sinful disciples into ardent apostles and martyrs, freed of all selfishness. By the Spirit of the risen Lord Jesus they were healed of sin and learned progressively to live for Christ.

Ultimately it is only God who gives life and only he can "regenerate" you. He is "Yahweh who heals" (Ex 15:26) and he heals through his Son, Jesus Christ, who extends himself into this broken world by means of his body, the church. In personal and communal prayer Jesus can still touch you profoundly in any kind or degree of brokenness and lead you into a newness of sharing his risen life. In the sacraments, especially the rite of reconciliation and the Eucharist, he encounters you in your darkness and leads you into the light of his healing presence.

He meets you as you pray holy scripture under the guidance of his Spirit. His word can ignite in your heart a spark of new faith, hope and love that will hurtle you beyond the confinement of your own self-contained world. His word has a freeing power that can truly set you free:

"If you make my word your home
you will indeed be my disciples,
you will learn the truth
and the truth will make you free" (Jn 8:31-32).

Jesus Heals   When Jesus confronted the broken ones — the maimed, the blind, lepers, paralytics, epileptics, the possessed, sinners living in the darkness of selfishness, bound by pride, hatred and self-indulgence — his love and compassionate mercy went out to them. He was the imaged-love of the Father suffering to see his children suffer. So he healed all of them, provided they believed in him and accepted him as the Lord of their lives.

If the broken ones whom he met accepted his love, the

almighty love of the Father's Spirit reflected through the beautiful humanity of Christ, they were set free from their slavery to live freely in giving that same Spirit of love to others.

Your broken condition, regardless of the causes or degrees of intensity, can be healed by Jesus Christ. There is a way out of your inauthentic living. Jesus is that way, truth and life (Jn 14:6); even today he can heal you and set you free. Any obstacle in your life that hardens your heart into selfishness can be removed by him if you cry out to him in faith.

> "Have faith in God. I tell you solemnly, if anyone says to this mountain, 'Get up and throw yourself into the sea,' with no hesitation in his heart but believing that what he says will happen, it will be done for him. I tell you therefore: everything you ask and pray for, believe that you have it already, and it will be yours. And when you stand in prayer, forgive whatever you have against anybody, so that your Father in heaven may forgive your failings too" (Mk 11:23-25).

Prayerful Healing   You really do believe that Jesus Christ lives within you. Both he and his Father abide within you through the Spirit of the risen Lord Jesus (Jn 14:23). In the depths of your heart, as you silence the noise of all selfish clamorings within you, you can cry out to him with confidence: "Lord, Jesus Christ, Son of God, have mercy on me, a sinner!"

Jesus from within releases his Spirit of love. His Spirit inundates your heart, your consciousness, with the healing love of Jesus who loves you with an everlasting love, even to the last drop of blood poured out in the eternal now of his sacrifice on the cross. With St. Paul (Ga 2:20) you, too, can in awesome wonderment cry out: "For me Jesus dies!"

Today bring all of your brokenness to Jesus. Let his

tender but strong love fall gently on the hardness of your heart. Feel his warm presence surrounding you from all sides, in all your broken relationships. Bring to him any hurtful experiences of your past and present. Surrender all such pains received from others, especially from those who claimed a special place in your love.

See Jesus bending over you in those burdensome memories of yesteryear. Feel the heaviness gradually lift, leaving you light and free. See yourself being healed and made whole. Thank God for Jesus, the way! Praise him who is making you whole. Let God's nascent life flow through you. Hear Jesus cry out as he did to the entombed Lazarus (Jn 11:44): "Come out of your dark prison! I am making you whole! Let go of your bonds and chains that hold you mercilessly to the past. I am setting you free!"

Walk out of the dark cavern of self-confinement into the fresh spring sunlight of God's healing love. You were broken, but Jesus has healed you by your faith in his infinite love. You have surrendered to him and received the healing love that has always been there at the door of your heart.

Meditation

1. Place yourself in the dark tomb with Lazarus (Jn 11:38-44). Let Jesus unbind you and set you free. Let his deep love for you be experienced as the only, ultimate healing power in your condition of brokenness.

2. In the presence of the Trinity, Father, Son and Spirit, pray for healing of memories of the past. Let the loving Spirit of the risen Jesus enter into those painful relationships and bring you into newness of life.

3. Today would be an opportune time to receive the sacrament of reconciliation.

THIRD DAY

Jesus—the Way to the Father

One of the most devastating human experiences is that of *loneliness.* Have you ever been so lonely that you felt there was not one human being on earth who loved you and truly cared for you? You longed for someone to understand, to listen and to give a bit of affirmation, and no one called or knocked on your door. We are all, from time to time, caught in such doldrums that we begin to doubt whether we will ever escape.

Now project this human feeling of isolation upon the whole human race. God created us to live in communion with him in prayerful adoration and creative submission. But we, individually and as a part of the human race, hid from God. We closed our hearts to his presence. Like Cain, we "left the presence of Yahweh" (Gn 4:16) and traveled far, east of Eden. Desirous of love for God and neighbor, we pathetically strove to take love by force, only to force ourselves deeper into isolation and loneliness.

God's Merciful Plan   Yet God had mercy on his lonely children. He freely poured out his love into his only-begotten Son so that in the human form of God's Word made flesh we might possess the way to be reconciled to our heavenly Father.

> We all were among them too in the past, living sensual lives, ruled entirely by our own physical desires and our own ideas;

so that by nature we were as much under God's anger as the rest of the world. But God loved us with so much love that he was generous with his mercy: when we were dead through our sins, he brought us to life with Christ — it is through grace that you have been saved — and raised us up with him and gave us a place with him in heaven, in Christ Jesus (Ep 2:3-6).

We have wandered away from God but the Good Shepherd, Christ, picks us up on his shoulders and carries us back to the waiting arms of his Father. We go back to God only through Christ and with Christ. "I am the Way, the Truth and the Life. No one can come to the Father except through me" (Jn 14:6). Since Christ's coming, there is but one way to go to the Father: by, with and through Christ. Since Christ's coming, to praise, reverence and serve God means one thing: to know Christ more intimately, love him more ardently and follow him more closely.

Yet this was not an "added" plan to the frustration of the original plan of creation to live in communion with God. God from all eternity poured the fullness of divinity into Jesus Christ (Col 2:9). In God's view, the trinitarian relationships of the Father giving himself totally to the Son and calling him into being, and his Son receiving the fullness of the gift of the Father through the loving Spirit that bonded the Father and the Son together were meant to be the perfect model of the Trinity's relationships with us. The Father in the order of salvation seeks always to love only one person in total self-surrender and that person is his only Son. Yet in his Son, his logos, the Father speaks all of us into being as a part of his Son. The total Christ was meant to be Christ, God-man, united with every man and woman created through God's loving Spirit, adoring the Father in eternal praise, reverence and loving service.

The incarnation is not an afterthought of God that attempts to save something of his original plan which was frustrated through humans' sin. It is the culmination of God's self-giving.

> Yes, God loved the world so much
> that he gave his only Son,
> so that everyone who believes in him may not be lost
> but may have eternal life.
> For God sent his Son into the world
> not to condemn the world,
> but so that through him the world might be saved (Jn 3:16-17).

Jesus Still Alive   The incarnation, however, is not the end of God's plan. Jesus Christ, true God and true man, "pitched his tent among us" in order that we might accept his love, his Spirit, and receive in that infinite love the "power to become children of God" (Jn 1:12).

> When the appointed time came, God sent his Son, born of a woman, born a subject of the Law, to redeem the subjects of the Law and to enable us to be adopted as sons. The proof that you are sons is that God has sent the Spirit of his Son into our hearts: the Spirit that cries, "Abba, Father," and it is this that makes you a son, you are not a slave any more; and if God has made you son, then he has made you heir (Ga 4:4-7).

Jesus freely lays down his life for us in an excruciating emptying, even to the last drop of blood. Passing over from his own isolation and self-containment by the power of the Spirit, Jesus dies but is raised up by the Father's Spirit into a "new creation." By the "game of the resurrection," to use Teilhard de Chardin's phrase, he has inserted himself wondrously into the human race and the material world to be forever among us, drawing us into his body, forming us through the same Spirit that raised him from the dead into a new existence of glory, into his church that we might have a share with him in the kingdom of his Father.

Thus, in the rest of the retreat, Jesus is to be seen as still touching us as he touched the broken ones of his world. The towns of Galilee are to be replaced by our cities and countries of today, yet Jesus Christ is the same yesterday, today and always. By his resurrectional presence he lives within you and me and through us he can extend his healing, loving presence into the rest of the broken world that we touch by our physical and spiritual presence. Jesus has need of other human beings to become his body, his hands and feet, his members whereby he can bring "all things to be reconciled through him and for him, everything in heaven and everything on earth" (Col 1:20).

Let your prayer the rest of the retreat be centered on St. Paul's beautiful words:

> Out of his infinite glory, may he give you the power through his Spirit for your hidden self to grow strong, so that Christ may live in your hearts through faith and then planted in love and built on love, you will with all the saints have strength to grasp the breadth and the length, the height and the depth, until, knowing the love of Christ which is beyond all knowledge, you are filled with the utter fullness of God (Ep 3:16-19).

I: *Jesus Is King*

We cannot fall in love with God and surrender our whole life to his dominion unless he becomes very real to us. He cannot come close to us, at least this is the logic of God, unless he communicates vividly with us. For this reason God's Word becomes flesh in order to speak to us in human terms about the infinite beauty of the hidden, invisible God. But, more so, in Jesus Christ, God-incarnated, we not only receive words about God, we are able to make contact with the living Word of God who is not only the medium of God's revelation, but the message itself. Jesus Christ is the good news. The gospel is a person. By his Spirit, Jesus is able to reveal himself to us as risen and living within us, drawing us by his eternal love-act of dying for us. He is a dynamic, transforming power living within us.

St. Paul beautifully summarizes for you the dignity of this man, Jesus Christ:

> He is the image of the unseen God
> and the first-born of all creation,
> for in him were created
> all things in heaven and on earth:
> everything visible and everything invisible,
> Thrones, Dominations, Sovereignties, Powers —
> all things were created through him and for him.
> Before anything was created, he existed,
> and he holds all things in unity.
> Now the Church is his body,
> he is its head.
> . . . God wanted all perfection
> to be found in him
> and all things to be reconciled through him and for him (Col 1:15-19).

This most beautiful person of all the sons of men still lives and walks into your life. He still calls you to have a share with him in loving union along with the Father and his Spirit. But he also calls you to be healed of your brokenness by his personal love for you in order that you may offer yourself as a channel for his healing love, to go out and touch others in your world so that they too may enter the kingdom of his Father.

The Kingdom of God   The message of Jesus, which we see presented consistently on the pages of the New Testament gospels, touches three areas: Jesus announces the coming of the kingdom of God; he declares that both he and his followers must "die"; he promises that both he and they will share in the glory of the resurrection.

The good news that Jesus and his disciples preached is that the kingdom of God is now happening through Jesus himself. The "in-breaking" of the Father's tender love for each individual is now taking place as the individual accepts the lordship of Jesus and believes that he is truly one with the eternal Father.

> After John had been arrested, Jesus went into Galilee. There he proclaimed the Good News from God. "The time has come," he said, "and the kingdom of God is close at hand. Repent, and believe the Good News" (Mk 1:14-15).

This was the good news that Jesus was announcing to those who heard him during his lifetime on earth and the same good news he announces to you today. He is telling you that his loving Father has infinite mercy and forgiveness for you, is bringing healing love to your loneliness and isolation, is holding out hope to you in all your hopelessness. All this is imaged in this person, Jesus Christ. The in-breaking of God's loving relationships with you through his uncreated energies of love is being brought about by this man, Jesus.

A Worldly Kingdom   God had prepared his people for the message that his reign in their lives would be similar to a kingdom. He was worthy of their complete submission and obedience for he was their sovereign Lord.

> Yours, Yahweh, is the greatness, the power, splendor, length of days, glory, for all that is in the heavens and on the earth is yours. Yours is the sovereignty, Yahweh; you are exalted over all, supreme. Riches and honor go before you, you are ruler of all, in your hand lie strength and power; in your hand it is to give greatness and strength to all. At this time, our God, we give you glory, we praise the splendor of your name (1 Ch 29:11-13).

Gradually the Israelites lost the message of the kingdom

of God and replaced it with a temporal kingdom of worldly power and material prosperity. The Jews in the time of Christ, therefore, had been expecting the Messiah to come, but he would be one according to their worldly ambitions. They had forgotten the Old Testament prophecies of Isaiah and Jeremiah about the Messiah or the Son of Man who would come as the Suffering Servant of Yahweh.

Even the disciples of Jesus were looking for the restoration of the temporal kingdom of Israel. They were not ready to embrace the "wisdom" of God, so different from that of the world.

A Needed Conversion   Jesus would not yield to the expectations of his people in bringing about the kingdom of God. Jesus insisted over and over, amid much persecution and finally death itself, that he was a king of the kingdom and that he had the power to bring about a new relationship between human beings and God's loving presence. But this was possible only if people were converted in their hearts and would become humble enough to accept Jesus and the scandal of the cross.

> "I tell you solemnly, unless you change and become like little children you will never enter the kingdom of heaven. And so, the one who makes himself as little as this little child is the greatest in the kingdom of heaven" (Mt 18:3-4).

He was asking his disciples—and is asking you today—to turn away from self-centeredness by a *metanoia* or inner conversion. In Greek this word means that one have a complete turnabout in one's consciousness. The values by which one lives must now be centered completely on God as manifested through the workings of God's Word, Jesus Christ. St. Paul calls it a "spiritual revolution" (Ep 4:23). Jesus himself insisted that we must be "reborn" of his Spirit or we cannot enter the kingdom of God:

ALONE WITH THE ALONE

"I tell you most solemnly,
unless a man is born from above,
he cannot see the kingdom of God.
. . . unless a man is born through water and the Spirit,
he cannot enter the kingdom of God" (Jn 3:3,5).

A Gentle Spirit   To receive God's life within us, Jesus says, we must embrace a different kind of wisdom. This wisdom is revealed only to the little ones, those who are poor in spirit.

"My soul proclaims the greatness of the Lord
and my spirit exults in God my saviour;
because he has looked upon his lowly handmaid"
(Lk 1:46-47).
"How happy are the poor in spirit;
theirs is the kingdom of heaven" (Mt 5:3).

The love relationships between the Trinity of Father, Son and Holy Spirit and us are brought about when we have that spiritual poverty, another word for humility, that empties us of power and self-containment and opens us up to God's free gift of himself.

"I am also with the contrite and humbled spirit,
to give the humbled spirit new life,
to revive contrite hearts" (Is 57:15).

Jesus described in the parable of the sower (Mk 4:3-20) the gentle spirit that is needed if we are to allow God to enter into our lives. God's word is the seed that falls into our hearts; we receive it with varying dispositions. Some of us have a "hardened" disposition like soil on a path. The seed cannot take root. Others receive the word of God but there are rocks in the soil and the rocks prevent the seed from sinking deep roots into the earth. Still others are filled with worldly cares and anxieties and are like soil which bears thorny plants and weeds that choke the tender sprouts. You, however, are to hear the word of God as earth, broken and

68

ready to receive it with complete obedience. You will enter into the kingdom of God, into a living relationship with the Trinity.

Conditions for Entering the Kingdom   Jesus was the greatest of realists. He knew what was in the heart of us humans. But more importantly, he came into our human existence so that he could be one with our heart. By dying ignominiously on the cross through the shedding of his blood to the last drop, his Father raised him in glory by his Spirit of love and in his risen life he is now able to be ever present to you. In the Spirit that he wishes to release in your heart, he is pouring out his infinite and ever-the-same love for you. And in that tender drawing of your heart into his you are called to leave your false self and enter into your true being by becoming united, one with Christ. In a word, Jesus risen gives you his Spirit who makes it possible to become regenerated into his new life. His Spirit allows you to live your Christian baptism of death-resurrection.

There are only two choices: you serve either God or Mammon, your own selfishness as though you were the center of your world, or your God. Either you choose death and a life of meaninglessness by cutting yourself off from God's life within you, or you choose life and a share in the resurrectional glory even now, as you allow Jesus to be your Lord and master, king of your universe. But this union with Jesus cannot come about unless you are ready to enter into a dying process.

> I tell you, most solemnly,
> unless a wheat grain falls on the ground and dies,
> it remains only a single grain;
> but if it dies,
> it yields a rich harvest.
> Anyone who loves his life loses it;

anyone who hates his life in this world
will keep it for the eternal life.
If a man serves me, he must follow me,
wherever I am, my servant will be there too.
If anyone serves me, my Father will honor him (Jn 12:24-26).

If You Wish   The first condition that Jesus holds out to us
is an appeal to our free-will following of him. It is a gentle invitation with no force or coercion whatsoever. "If you wish"
means that it is up to you to choose. Do you wish to share in
his life? You can freely choose death rather than life by
choosing to remain alone.

Many throughout the history of Christianity have
wanted to be followers of Christ up to a point, that is, until it
began to cost. Jesus said that not everyone who says "Lord,
Lord," will enter his kingdom, but only those who keep his
commandments. The rich man in the gospel story wanted to
follow Jesus. Jesus thrilled at his goodness: "Jesus looked
steadily at him and loved him" (Mk 10:21). Yet Jesus
challenged him to give up his identity formed through riches
and to find his true self in total dependence upon him. The
paradox, to choose poverty in order to obtain the complete
richness that could never be taken from him was beyond his
comprehension. He wanted to follow Jesus with his affec-
tions but he was not ready to give up all in order to possess
all in Jesus.

> "There is one thing you lack. Go and sell everything you own
> and give the money to the poor, and you will have treasure
> in heaven; then come, follow me." But his face fell at these
> words and he went away sad, for he was a man of great
> wealth (Mk 10:21-22).

Deny Yourself   In the synoptic gospels of Matthew, Mark
and Luke the conditions for following Jesus are repeated in a
similar fashion, always including the crucial accent on self-

denial or death to one's self-centeredness. St. Mark gives the essence of the doctrine, which is repeated by the other two synoptics:

> "If anyone wants to be a follower of mine, let him renounce himself and take up his cross and follow me. For anyone who wants to save his life will lose it; but anyone who loses his life for my sake and for the sake of the gospel, will save it" (Mk 8:34; Mt 10:38, 16:24; Lk 9:23, 14:27).

Perhaps you have heard in your spiritual training all too much about carrying the cross. You believe that your Lord is a risen Lord. But the message of the gospel is that there is no sharing in the resurrection of Jesus, whereby we live in love toward God and others, unless there is also a death to self, as Jesus showed us. "This, in fact, is what you were called to do, because Christ suffered for you and left an example for you to follow the way he took" (1 P 2:21).

We believe that, if we could only get rid of this physical suffering, receive a better-paying job, get an annulment, we would be better able to serve the Lord. The disciples of Jesus could not comprehend the mystery of evil and suffering and sought to have the first place of honor without any suffering and humiliation.

> And so, while the Jews demand miracles and the Greeks look for wisdom, here are we preaching a crucified Christ; to the Jews an obstacle that they cannot get over, to the pagans madness, but to those who have been called, whether they are Jews or Greeks, a Christ who is the power and the wisdom of God. For God's foolishness is wiser than human wisdom, and God's weakness is stronger than human strength (1 Cor 1:23-25).

After his resurrection, Jesus is found patiently teaching his disciples the mystery of the cross. "You foolish men! So slow to believe the full message of the prophets! Was it not ordained that the Christ should suffer and so enter into his glory?" (Lk 24:26). The mystery of death-resurrection must

71

be understood sufficiently so that we can embrace the cross in the hope of entering into a new loving relationship with the glorified Christ, and we will have that understanding only if the Spirit of the risen Jesus is enlightening us as to the depths of the love Jesus has for us. Such a call to our true identity allows us to bear all things, whether they come actually from the pruning hand of the Father or through his permissive will operating in the actions of other persons.

In the teaching of Jesus and the experience of the early martyrs the cross was not a stumbling block but the very means through which Jesus would be able to touch us and prove to us through the Spirit that he and the Father have the same eternal, infinite love for us. The cross for us is meaningful only insofar as it spells a dying to self-centeredness and a rising into a new oneness with Christ where he alone guides us through his Spirit of love. By the power of this loving Spirit we can grow into a desire for creative suffering, to go another mile, all because that is the standard by which Jesus lived. If we wish to have a share with him in glory; then we wish also a share in his death: "It would be a sign from God that he has given you the privilege not only of believing in Christ, but of suffering for him as well" (Ph 1:29).

And Follow Me   Jesus is calling you to share in his sufferings so that you might share in his glory. He goes first, pointing the way to Calvary which typifies the peak of self-giving in total emptying for love of the other. It is amazing what you can do when the inspiration is great enough. It is impossible to go against your false self at all times and put on the mind of Christ unless you are experiencing at each moment his immense love, very present within you, calling you to a like generosity.

Jesus tells you that he has taken upon himself all that you will ever be asked to bear. He asks you to let go of your fears and anxieties and trust in his strength working within you in your weakness. With St. Paul you learn what the words of Christ in your daily life of suffering mean: "My grace is enough for you: my power is at its best in weakness" (2 Cor 12:9). With St. Paul you discover in following Jesus that ". . . it is when I am weak that I am strong" (2 Cor 12:10).

Your Response   Your response to the greatest cause in the world (even though you may not feel sincere in making the response) is to want to follow Jesus and share somewhat in his sufferings that are a result of true love for others. What response will you give to your leader and king? Look at the mangled face of your Lord as he hangs on the cross. He turns to you. Hear his loving invitation to come and do battle with him. He does not command; he invites you. And the reward is: "Today you will be with me in paradise" (Lk 23:43).

Not only is he calling you to purify your heart of all selfishness and to allow him to enter into your life as your king and Lord, but he is asking your permission to take your hands and feet, your eyes, your tongue, your whole being, in order that he might work through you to bring others to know of the great love of the Father as mirrored forth by his Son in his Spirit. He is giving you work that only you can do to establish the kingdom of God on this earth. Surely you should at least want to follow such a leader as Christ!

Speak to him today and tell him, in spite of any repugnance or fear of suffering and accepting the crosses that will come to you as a consequence of following him in all things, that you really want to side with him, to stand next to him, sharing in his sufferings so as to enter into glory. If bearing hardships, poverty, rejections by others are to be a sharing in his sufferings, then tell him in your weakness that you are ready. If he is with you, who can be against you?

73

This is the greatest privilege of your life: standing next to Christ, your king, to do battle against the prince of this world.

Meditation

Place yourself before the bloodstained, humiliated Christ as he stands before Pontius Pilate. The latter asks him, "Are you the king of the Jews?" (Lk 23:3). Ponder prayerfully what kind of a king Jesus is for you. Let him tell you how you are to enter into his kingdom (Mk 8:34-38). Hear him describe the love relationship he wishes to establish with you. He wishes also to work through your ministry to bring others into such happiness and fulfillment. Offer to follow his standard of poverty, ready if need be, to accept rejection and humiliation, all in order that he might be completely Lord and master in your life and that you might live humbly in love and service to him and your neighbor.

II: *The Hidden Life*

A thing difficult for most Christians is to understand that Jesus was totally human. He was the pre-existent Word of God that became flesh. Yet he lived most of his life in obscurity in Nazareth as the son of a humble carpenter, Joseph. He was as human as you are and, therefore, subject to all human laws of growth. "And Jesus increased in wisdom, in stature, and in favor with God and men" (Lk 2:52). He had a human body, as you have, with its physical and psychic parts. He hungered and thirsted, required sleep, had sexual powers which he needed to discipline along with intellectual, emotional and volitional endowments: "We have one who has been tempted in every way that we are, though he is without sin" (Heb 4:15).

It is good on this day of the retreat to place yourself mentally at Nazareth and fill yourself with the spirit of Jesus. Go there to learn God's values over the values of the world: "Now the life you have is hidden with Christ in God" (Col 3:3). Jesus, from his humble birth in a cave at Bethlehem and throughout his simple life at Nazareth, as well as in the public life that led to his hour of death on the cross, teaches you in what human greatness consists.

According to worldly standards he was "getting nowhere fast." Buried away in an insignificant corner of Galilee, Jesus lived a life of complete surrender in love to his heavenly Father. He had to learn to live humanly with his own divinity. He had to discover in every facet of his humanity the presence of God and to yield that part of his being in loving obedience to his Father. He had to learn to let God be God as he tempered his human will to the divine power that was at his command. It would be his human hands that would touch a leper and heal him, and that experience of using his hands in loving touch was an experience he had to learn. His human voice would cry out and Lazarus would come from the grave. His human intelligence that pondered over the scriptures of his ancestors in his village synagogue would be the instrument for communicating God's divine message to human beings. He had to study that message and experience it in the marrow of his bones.

Task at Nazareth That is what took place at Nazareth. He had to grow into a fully realized personality that would be totally human, yet totally submissive to the divine Father whom he progressively experienced in his humanity as dwelling intimately within him, making him and the Father one (Jn 17:21). He left Nazareth when he was ready, tradition tells us about his 30th year of life, and we are amazed that he had accomplished his task so quickly. He was not

75

wasting his time at Nazareth. He was preparing for the redemption of the world!

What happened at Nazareth is a pattern for what must happen in you. You have God dwelling within you. God the Father, Son and Holy Spirit have united themselves to your humanity. Your principal task while in this earthly existence is to learn progressively how to discover this indwelling Trinity within you and outside of you, working dynamically out of love for you with its uncreated energies of love at each moment and in each event. You are to see God shining diaphanously, first, from within the depths of your being. "Didn't you realize that you were God's temple and that the Spirit of God was living among you? If anybody should destroy the temple of God, God will destroy him, because the temple of God is sacred; and you are that temple" (1 Cor 3:16-17).

Your life is a lifelong Nazareth that you spend in exploring, or at least in seeking to explore the deepest parts of yourself where God dwells. You will never fully reach that level of intimacy or of self-surrender to the Trinity since there is an infinity of surrender and greater union that can be attained. You have to learn how to use your imagination, intellect, emotions, will, sexuality, your entire body-soul-spirit being in loving gift to God who is intimately present and giving himself, Father, Son and Spirit, to you. If God is present within you, he is there as activated energies of love. He moves within you with his personalistic love relationships as Father, Son and Spirit. If this is true on a faith level, it is meant to be an experience of divine movement within your life with your continued response the same as Jesus made throughout his entire earthly life: "Not my will, but yours be done."

The End of Life   The end of your life, as of the human existence of Jesus, is to move freely according to the inspirations of the Holy Spirit who dwells within you. It is to bring yourself completely through the Spirit into complete obedience to Jesus Christ and his heavenly Father who dwell within you. It is to structure and discipline your body, soul and spirit relationships that you move with authentic directness in the power of the Spirit through the Son of the Father. This can be expressed briefly as familiarity with God.

The humanity of Jesus acquired this familiarity at Nazareth. Jesus moved his human consciousness and all his human powers directly through the indwelling Spirit to total oneness with the Father. Jesus in his humanity became one with his divinity and that oneness brought him into oneness with the Father through the same Holy Spirit. You are not divine by nature but by God's permeating, uncreated energies of love that we can call "primal grace." Your aim in life is to join your humanity in oneness with the permeating, divine, triune Persons who dwell within you. It means the ability to find God easily in all things. It means sensitivity to his presence. It means contentedness in abiding in God. It means docility to all movements of his Spirit.

It means straightness and truth in the movement of your intentions to please God in every thought, word and deed. It means that you allow yourself willingly to be caught up in the total current of God's powerful love flowing strongly, gently throughout all your life. It means that you have "interior eyes" to see how all events, even those the world may label insignificant or unpleasant, can be exciting points of unveiling the loving presence of God, allowing you to become more a participator in God's own divine nature (2 P 1:4).

This is the goal of your life. The growth is slow and even painful. But if you realize what the aim of your life is and that in growing toward this goal you are imitating in a very profound way your blessed Lord, then you will give yourself joyously and generously to attaining this goal.

A Poor and Simple Life   Jesus led a very simple life. The poor villagers in a town like Nazareth during the time of Jesus lived with only the mere necessities. Jesus' poverty was more than physical. He entered into a psychic and spiritual poverty in his humanity that reflected his basic, divine attitude toward his heavenly Father within the Trinity. As the eternal Son of God, he realized that everything he possessed was sheer gift from the love of the Father. In his humanity Jesus continually reflected this relationship. And according to this likeness all of us have been created. Jesus in his humanity experienced daily at Nazareth and throughout his earthly life that he was most radically and ontologically nonbeing except for God's outpoured love in unselfish creation.

As Jesus experienced, through the Father's Spirit, the riches of God poured out first into his humanity, he lived poverty. Such poverty became for him a humble recognition of God's sovereignty and free gift of his love. It is a permanent attitude of mind that Jesus assumed toward himself, his Father and each person whom he met. It is a poverty that can be called humility. Jesus is nothing in his human creation. The Father is all. His Son is meek and humble of heart (Mt 11:29). Jesus surrenders himself to do whatever the Father wishes him to do, both at Nazareth and on the cross.

Jesus was poor. He lived as a carpenter in a small village and as an itinerant preacher dependent on the goodwill offerings of others for food and shelter. He was not destitute or heroic in his poverty. But he was absolutely poor because no *thing* possessed him. He was possessed only by his Father and so he used things only as an external expression of that inner emptiness before the all-ness of his Father.

A Life of Hard Work   There are few of us who escape from earning a living by our work. Before the first man had fallen through disobedience, God had already given him the command to take this created world and fashion it into a song of praise to its creator: "Be fruitful, multiply, fill the earth and conquer. Be masters of the fish of the sea, the birds of heaven and all living animals on the earth" (Gn 1:28). Yet we find so often that our work is not so beautifully creative. We do not always seem to be developing ourselves or the universe into something noble and creative by our humdrum work, but rather our work becomes all too often very banal and monotonous, even boring.

The life of Jesus hidden away in a carpenter shop at Nazareth could hardly be called "creative" in the sense of modern psychology. Jesus had to labor diligently for the simple things that he and his family needed to sustain them in life. The power that he had at hand was his own brawn and muscle. He had to sweat much in the Galilean heat. And after a full day's work, what were his recreations? He did not have any of the modern devices that amuse and recreate us. His life was one continuous round of monotonous duties. At night the glow of a candle or small oil lamp for a few hours more until he fell into sleep only to return to the same work the next day.

One with the keen insights of the 20th century might surely ask: "Where was he going with his life? One day yielded to the next; one year to the other. The same neighbors, the same work, the same food. Stagnation had surely set in!" Yet it was the interior spirit of Jesus that transformed what appeared to be a life of no great creativity into a life of infinite beauty and value before his heavenly Father: "He who sent me is with me and has not left me to myself, for I always do what pleases him" (Jn 8:29).

The Spirit in Jesus allowed him to grow in each moment and in each activity of each event "in wisdom, in stature, and in favor with God and men" (Lk 2:52). All anxiety and boredom were removed from his openness to meet

79

his loving Father in each fresh moment. The situation was not objectified as either holy or profane, pleasant or unpleasant, worthwhile or worthless. But from the inner presence of the Spirit, he moved freely through life's events and circumstances to respond fully according to the Father's mind. His life, made up of each moment and his free choices within that moment, brought him into a growing experience that in all things he was the Word, one with the mind of the Father. Free from sin and self-seeking, Jesus was free in his work to be loved infinitely by his Father and to strive in the context of the work of his daily life to respond joyfully in a return of that love.

Whether Jesus was lying on a slope outside Nazareth watching the fleecy clouds pass by in ever-changing creations of beauty, or transforming wood into things needed by his neighbors, he found his Father's loving presence and praised him in joyful surrender. His daily work was a way of acting out his devotion to his Father. Each action was important as he labored in all things to please the Father. Each moment was a labor of love, a song of self-surrender.

Jesus Obedient　　We read these words: "He then went down with them and came to Nazareth and lived under their authority" (Lk 2:51). Day after day, like any other child in any other Jewish home of that time, Jesus lived and performed the slightest wish or command of Joseph and Mary and in that obedience he discovered the wish of his heavenly Father. He obeyed them in everything that they wished him to do. He surely could not say that the Father was leading him exactly as those in authority around him commanded him, yet he knew that the Father would be discovered in those social relationships as he accepted his place in that society of family and village.

As God loved his material world and sent his only-begotten Son to become forever a part of that world through the incarnation, so Jesus knew that the material world, especially the interaction of human beings, would be the "place" where his heavenly Father would speak to him of his eternal love and allow Jesus to make his return of love to the Father. Jesus was obedient to others in legitimate authority because in his gentle spirit he was always present to his Father who spoke to him through others. The Father was greater than he and without the Father the Son could do nothing (Jn 5:30; 14:28). This Father, he knew, was always working (Jn 5:17) and Jesus sought to work with him. Yet Jesus was no automaton. He had to search to discover what would most please the Father and this brought him into an obedience to the Father by obeying others.

In the depths of his heart, his innermost consciousness, Jesus touched the Holy. He breathed, smiled, laughed and cried in the holy presence of his infinitely loving Father. All outside creatures, touching Jesus in new, surprising experiences, were received as gifts by that delicate, sensitive gentleness in him. When Jesus gave himself up to obey others, it was a joyful act of freedom to take his life in hand and return it totally and freely back to his Father. Seeking only his Father's will, Jesus was able to obey others because he sought only to obey his Father.

The Prayer of Jesus   Go down to Nazareth to learn how to live your life in the spirit of the hidden years of Jesus. Learn from him how to pray. Jesus lived what he taught his disciples: "But when you pray, go to your private room and, when you have shut your door, pray to your Father who is in that secret place and your Father who sees all that is done in secret will reward you" (Mt 6:6).

When Jesus spoke in Aramaic about prayer, he used the words *zla* and *zlotha*. Prayer in this sense means to tune in to the wavelength of God. Jesus at Nazareth prayed in the sense of always walking in the communicating presence of his Father. He sought to bring his consciousness in loving surrender to the consciousness of the Father, who was always present, seeking communion with his Son through his Spirit of love.

Jesus teaches you that prayer is fundamentally, therefore, a listening to God as he continually communicates his love to you at each moment. We pray when we are "attentive" to the presence of God, when we lift up our heart and our mind to God's communicating presence. God does not begin and then cease to enter into this self-giving. His Son, Jesus, at Nazareth, realized that his Father surrounded him at every moment of his earthly existence with his Spirit. He opened himself to receive that "invasion" of his Father by yielding actively to whatever the Father was asking of him at each moment. Thus Jesus prayed always in whatever he was engaged in doing.

He had to discover each day that his very activities were to be the "place" in secret where he was to tune into the Father's loving presence. Unlike us, who so often find our work a distraction that takes us away from being attentive to the presence of God, Jesus received the loving "invasion" of his Father at each moment.

In such a state of inner attentiveness to the Father's loving energies in each event, Jesus learned that true prayer is ultimately union of wills with the Father whom he loved in return for the infinite, ever-present love of his Father toward him. At Nazareth in his humanity he learned that the quality of his prayer was not measured by how great he felt in prayer but rather how surrendered he was in his will-determination to be total gift to the Father.

Prayer for Jesus became not an activity that he engaged in before he did something else, but it was a state of being turned inwardly toward the Father at every moment in loving adoration and self-surrender. Prayer became synonymous with love. "My son, give me your heart" (Pr 23:26—CV).

Such *heartful,* loving surrender meant *devotion* of Jesus toward the Father. True devotedness in Jesus and in our love for God and friend means always a turning toward the one we love in total vulnerability and sheer gift to dispose ourselves in whatever the beloved asks of us. Jesus learned the devotion toward the Father that he would manifest throughout his public life, especially in his agony and death on the cross, at Nazareth in the quiet hours of monotony as he turned inwardly in formal prayer and throughout the day in his busy activities of work, to the indwelling Father and surrendered to him so that every thought, word and deed flowed from that surrendering love.

A Trinitarian Community   Jesus preached that eternal life was in knowing the indwelling community of Father and Son in the Spirit of love: "And eternal life is this: to know you, the only true God, and Jesus Christ whom you have sent" (Jn 17:3). Through God's Word Incarnate, therefore, the one "nearest the heart of the Father" (Jn 1:18), God reveals to you his inner life. This revealing Word, Jesus Christ, by his death and resurrection, is now a living Word, dwelling within you along with his Holy Spirit. He not only gives you the elements that constitute God's inner life as he experienced them in his prayer at Nazareth and throughout his entire life, but he makes it possible through his Spirit for those elements to be experienced by you.

This trinitarian community of Father, Son and Holy Spirit, constantly communicating itself to you at all times, is at the heart of all reality. You are a gift of that love. Your life is to share with Jesus at Nazareth more and more at each moment that mystery of love, that you may humbly share the secret of God's very own intimate life. This reality, Jesus shows you at Nazareth, is meant by God to be experienced. Your life is to be one with that of Jesus at Nazareth, hidden in the tremendous reality of God's triune, personalized love for you at each moment. St. Paul beautifully summarizes the goal of your prayer life:

> Let your thoughts be on heavenly things, not on the things on the earth, because you have died and now the life you have is hidden with Christ in God. But when Christ is revealed and he is your life you too will be revealed in all your glory with him (Col 3:3).

Meditation

Go down to Nazareth and there contemplate Jesus in his hidden life (Lk 2:39-40, 51-52). Fernandez in his *Life of Christ* gives us St. John Damascene's description of Christ: "Jesus is tall in stature, distinguished in appearance, commanding respect and inspiring both love and reverence. His hair, chestnut brown, and reaching to his shoulders . . . is parted in the middle after the manner of the Nazarenes. His forehead is smooth and serene. His face is handsome, slightly ruddy in complexion and without wrinkle or blemish. His beard is full . . . and forked at the chin. His eyes are clear and bluish in color. When he reproves, he is terrible to behold; when he admonishes he is kind and gentle. His whole bearing is joyful, yet grave. . . . He speaks little and then modestly. He is the most beautiful of the sons of men."

Let Jesus reveal to you in this contemplation on his hidden life how he led a life of:
1. poverty
2. hard work
3. obedience
4. prayer.

What must your life be if your humanity is to become completely divinized by his Spirit?

III: *Speak, Lord, Your Servant Hears*

Jesus taught us that our true success story as Christians and human beings consists in seeking always to please our heavenly Father. St. Luke summarizes both the earthly life of Jesus as he strove to please his Father and our own earthly lives as we too must strive always to do the will of the Father when he narrates the finding of the child Jesus in the Temple.

After Mary and Joseph had grieved over his loss in their frantic searching for three days to find their lost child, Jesus simply replies with the answer that motivated his whole life: "Why were you looking for me? Did you not know that I must be busy with my Father's affairs?" (Lk 2:49-50).

Jesus declared that: "Anyone who does the will of my Father in heaven, he is my brother and sister and mother" (Mt 12:50). All his life Jesus strove to do the will of his Father because he knew and taught us that true love is proved by deeds and true action means seeking always to please the Father in everything he wishes.

But to say that Jesus did always the will of the Father admits of many levels of loving sensitivity. The most basic level of loving obedience to the will of his Father came in Jesus doing always what he knew was a clear expression of his will as a command: "Let your will be done, not mine" (Lk 22:43). There were many actions that Jesus felt he had to do in order to do the commands of the Father. At times, such as his terrifying agony in the Garden of Gethsemane and as he hung dying slowly on the cross of Calvary, these actions caused him great suffering.

As we also experience a higher level of sensitive love-response in seeking to go beyond mere commands to embrace whatever our loved ones would wish us to do, so Jesus strove also to do whatever he saw as a clear wish expressed by his Father. Commands are clearly expressed. To do the wish of another one has to be sensitively listening to the other express that wish in delicate ways. Jesus showed more love in seeking to do the will of his Father, which meant seeking to do at all times whatever he sensitively saw to be the mere expression of the Father's wish, than in the love he manifested in merely doing the commands of the Father.

Creative Suffering   Still, Jesus found, as we also realize in our human love relationships, that there is yet a higher level of doing the will of his Father. This consisted in going even beyond the expressed commands and the wishes delicately communicated to him by the Father's Spirit, to arrive at a state of love-response where he swung so freely in the love of the Father that he spontaneously strove to improvise ways of creatively proving his love: "He who sent me is with me, and has not left me to myself, for I always do what pleases him" (Jn 8:29).

On this level of "doing the will of the Father," there is no expressed manifestation of the Father's will one way or the other. No command or expressed wish directs Jesus to express his great love. It is sheerly out of the abundance of the love received from the Father that Jesus is moved to "invent" ways to express creatively his love for the Father. As the Father poured out the divinity of his being into his Son (Col 2:9), so Jesus strove to do things that would generate new levels of self-giving. Love is proved mostly by suffering, even unto death: "A man can have no greater love than to lay down his life for his friends" (Jn 15:13).

The heart of Christ is not impelled by any right or just claim upon him by the Father which would communicate a specific manner of how he must show his return of love. The Father breathes his Spirit into his Son and in substance tells him: "Anything you would wish to do to show your love for me would please me." But we know that in human language

86

what most communicates the level of love experienced and returned to the beloved is measured in terms of the cost to ourselves. Creative suffering is never an obligation. It is the peak of freedom in love to improvise, to do something that costs a price in personal suffering, in order to prove that love.

If St. Paul wanted to be co-crucified with Christ (Ga 2:19), even to bear in his body the marks of Christ's passion, what must have been the desire in the heart of Christ on the cross to return to the Father by creative suffering the infinite love that the Father poured out into him?

To Do the Will of God   Therefore, from the life of Christ we see that the goal of his life was to do always the will of his Father. But this was not a static message or something to do as received from the Father. It admitted of degrees that measured the sensitive intensity in love. Your goal in life is to seek always to pray effectively: "Our Father . . . thy kingdom come, thy will be done . . ." But what level of doing the Father's will are you concerned with? Do you seek to do only the commands, the great and clear injunctions that God imposes upon you in the Ten Commandments? Do you move sensitively in love to push yourself to listen to the Spirit revealing to you at each moment what the Father is wishing you to do? Surely this level of sensitivity in discerning the will of God demands great love to put aside your own rationalization and self-seeking to be constantly open to whatever God wishes you to do at any given moment.

But such a state of "passionate indifference," which inclines you to be so ready and prompt to embrace what you know would be the wish of the Father, cannot be a constant attitude unless from time to time you bring into your life a bit of the "heroic," a movement of the Spirit urging you to go beyond justice and to create your own symbols of love through creative suffering.

87

Building Generosity   God's Spirit speaks to you and draws
you to return the Father's love by seeking to do his will on
these three levels. You can hear the Spirit prompting you to
be in tune to discern the Father's will in many ways. The
Spirit can speak to you in holy scripture as to how to please
the Father as you read prayerfully the word of God. You can
listen to the word of God speaking to you in the context of
your daily life. You might receive a phone call or a letter
from a friend or have an ordinary conversation with a fellow
worker and in that event the Spirit could speak to you about
the will of the Father.

It is usually in the ordinary circumstances of your life
that the Spirit reveals to you the Father's great love and
moves you to want to return that love. However, if you are
not generously rooted in self-sacrifice, you will have no ability to discern the voice of the Holy Spirit. Before you can
hear what is God's will for you on any of the above-
mentioned levels of generosity, you will need to have a
habitual mind-set in the following three areas in order to put
you in an attitude of generosity.

The first is to live in anticipation of Jesus' promise to
release his Spirit within your life. Jesus promised to send his
Spirit to his disciples to teach them all about Jesus (Jn
14:25-27). That Spirit would make them witnesses
throughout the world (Jn 15:26-27). He would lead them to
complete truth (Jn 16:12-15). That same Spirit is promised
by Jesus to be with you always if only you ask and seek him
from the Father (Lk 11:9-13).

St. Paul urges you to know the will of God through the
release of the Spirit: "And do not be thoughtless but
recognize what is the will of the Lord . . . be filled with the
Spirit" (Ep 5:18). Your very bodies are temples of the indwelling Spirit (1 Co 3:16; 6:19). You need not fear that you
may not have that Spirit without whom there can be no
discernment of what would most please the Father. The

Spirit of God's great love dwells within you (Rm 8:9) and will surely lead you into all truth through right discernment if only you are sincere enough to rely on Jesus' promises that he will give you his Spirit to keep you from all error and sin.

Co-Crucified with Christ   The second attitude of mind you need to have is to die to self. You may want to know the will of God for you in any given circumstance, but unless you are ready to die to your own self-seeking there can be no true listening to the voice of the Spirit of love. Jesus himself so often repeated this necessary stage of generosity in order to become a sincere listener to his Spirit: "If anyone wants to be a follower of mine, let him renounce himself and take up his cross and follow me. For anyone who wants to save his life will lose it; but anyone who loses his life for my sake will find it" (Mt 16:24-25).

The Spirit will take over in your life to illumine you at each step in order to know the mind of God only if you remove from your life any resistance to Christ. Dying to your own controlled life and putting on Christ can come only if you are "tilted" toward the cross, toward a readiness to embrace suffering which usually will come as you seek to put aside your ways and replace them with the values of self-sacrificing love. St. Paul beautifully expresses how he lived in this attitude of generosity by his readiness to suffer anything in order that Jesus Christ live in him:

> I have been crucified with Christ, and I live now not with my own life but with the life of Christ who lives in me. The life I now live in this body I live in faith; faith in the Son of God who loved me and who sacrificed himself for my sake (Ga 2:19-20).

Jesus Is Your Lord   The third area of moving toward generosity and ready listening to God's Spirit in order to discern what the Father may be asking of you at any given moment is a state of honest sincerity to let Jesus be your unique Lord and Savior. How few of us at all times can repeat with full honesty what Mary said in summing up her entire life of self-surrender: "I am the handmaid of the Lord, let what you have said be done to me" (Lk 1:38).

It is this desire to allow Jesus to direct your life so that he is the living force from within that frees you from your own self-centeredness. It is yielding daily to the Holy Spirit whom Jesus releases within you and in that Spirit you can declare not only in words but in deeds that Jesus Christ is truly your Lord: "No one can say, 'Jesus is Lord' unless he is under the influence of the Holy Spirit" (1 Cor 12:3).

Without the Spirit of Jesus risen you cannot enter into the living of your first baptism that is always a death to sin and self-centeredness and a rising to a new oneness with Jesus Christ. It is not enough to profess with your lips that Jesus is Lord; you must proclaim this reality of his sovereignty over you by every thought, word and deed. If you truly wish to follow the will of God, you must be ready to discipline yourself so that everything about your life is brought under the lordship of Jesus. This requires a dying process of constant vigilance to bring everything about your life under Christ: "Every thought is our prisoner, captured to be brought into obedience to Christ. Once you have given your complete obedience, we are prepared to punish any disobedience" (2 Cor 10:5-6).

Thus if you are sincerely intent on letting Jesus Christ rule your life, you will be attentive at all times to the operating of the Spirit, showing you the proper way, the *holy* way, to act as befits a loving child of the heavenly Father. If you ask God to manifest to you what in the concrete details of your life would give him greater glory, you can rest assured that he will speak and give you the assurance in faith that you are under the guidance of his Spirit of love. Discernment is the sensitivity that is given to those who love the Lord with all their hearts to hear God's voice tell them what will most please him. Discernment is tied to love.

Meditation

Prayerfully ponder in the hidden life of Christ what St. Luke proposes as a model of Christ's entire human life: the story of Jesus found in the Temple at the age of twelve years (Lk 2:41-52). Here is your story, too. When you become of age as an adult in the spiritual life, you must "flesh out" your baptism received years before, usually in infancy. You must live to do the will of your heavenly Father. All else must be subservient to the great *shema:* "You shall love Yahweh your God with all your heart, with all your soul, with all your strength" (Dt 6:5).

Understand what doing the will of God means to you. See that such a goal of your life breaks down into three levels of seeking to do what the Father wants, depending upon the degree of love you wish to return to God who has infinitely loved you. To live generously, dead to self and alive to Christ, your life is to be one of continuously living your baptism as you experience the risen Lord becoming the standard of the value-system that determines how you will seek to please your Father in heaven. True discernment is a growth in purifying your love: "Happy the pure in heart: they shall see God" (Mt 5:8). They shall hear God speak his will and they will lovingly embrace that which they know will bring joy to the heart of their heavenly Father.

FOURTH DAY

Jesus, the Freest of All Persons

The work of Jesus is to bring us into greater and greater freedom as children of God. He still lives in his church, capable of touching us and freeing us by the love that he pours into our hearts through the Spirit whom he gives to us (Rm 5:5). He seeks to free us from our unreal selves by allowing us to know our real selves in loving relationship to him and the heavenly Father.

How do you know when you are free? True freedom, that which Jesus possessed, consists in freely determining to live your life as your heavenly Father would wish you to. It means that in all your choices you act out of love to please God. This freedom comes only as you experience God's love for you in Christ Jesus. It is a healing of your mistaken identity as you prayerfully encounter Jesus who loves you and breaks down your self-imposed prison walls.

Pray today and always for the grace to know Jesus more intimately, to love him more ardently and to follow him more closely. Seek to understand how attractive Jesus is in his freedom so that you may love him and receive his freeing power and be beautifully free in his love.

I: *Jesus Free*

Jesus was not free in a static manner. He grew into freedom as he sought daily during his earthly life to discover the face of his Father in each happening. Gerard Manley Hopkins, S.J., beautifully captures in poetry what must have been the attitude of Jesus as he was bathed in the loving presence of his Father:

> Thee, God, I come from
> To Thee, go.
> All day long I like fountain flow,
> From Thy hand out,
> Swayed about,
> Mote-like in Thy mighty glow!

The freedom of Jesus cannot be understood except in the light of the infinite love of the Father that was constantly poured out into his heart: "I am in the Father and the Father is in me" (Jn 14:11). "In his body lives the fullness of divinity" (Col 2:9), since the Father continually pours into his being the gift of himself in the Spirit of love. Joy, ecstasy, peace and happiness pour over Jesus as he not only receives the Father as gift but as he becomes a gift, freely given back in self-surrendering love to the Father.

Freedom was experienced in the long hours of deep, intimate prayer during the days and nights spent at Nazareth and during his public life. It was in such union that Jesus experienced the peak of human freedom. His freedom consisted in his prayer uttered in love and reverence for his Father: "Take, Lord, and receive, all my liberty, my whole life, all that I have or possess. It is all yours, do with it as you wish. Give me only your love; that is enough."

Nearest the Heart of the Father   Jesus was free because his life was rooted in his Father's loving presence permeating his entire being. Every atom in Jesus' being cried out in praise and joyous exultation to his Father, the source of his existence. Centered upon him, Jesus could face a world of multiplicity, of brokenness and of sin without losing his direction and scope in life. Although so much of the world that touched him was estranged from God and silenced by the lack of love into muted isolation, Jesus built his life in faith and was "planted in love" (Ep 3:18) of the Father.

Jesus was free in all his relationships because he was "nearest to the Father's heart" (Jn 1:18). He freely went about imaging the Father's love as he ministered God's tender mercy and healing to all the broken ones he met.

Free to Be Human   All of us have been made according to God's image and likeness. If, in the words of St. Irenaeus of the second century, "the glory of God is a man living fully," then Jesus surely must have lived fully as a human being. What freed him to be fully human and live for the glory of the Father in every human encounter was the vision he had of the omnipresence and constant loving activity of the Father in every moment of his earthly life.

Jesus said, "My Father goes on working, and so do I" (Jn 5:17). He lived his life in a oneness, a *symbiosis,* with the Father. Jesus saw the Father working out of love for him as he ate bread and drank wine, as he slept or rejoiced in the warm love of his friends. Nothing of the human situation could exclude the Father's loving activity.

Absent in the life of Jesus were the fitful moods or aggressive attacks upon others in order to have his own way. Gently Jesus opened himself as fully alive and completely human to encounter his Father in the fullness of his being. Therefore Jesus could be totally at home talking with the Samaritan woman at the well of Jacob or preaching to the multitudes. He was becoming more free as he freely took his life and returned it to his Father in joyful self-surrender.

Without Sin   Although Jesus entered into our broken condition and was "tempted in every way that we are" (Heb 4:15), he was entirely without sin. So convinced was Jesus of his complete oneness with the Father that he could challenge

95

the Pharisees: "Can one of you convict me of sin?" (Jn 8:46). In his sinlessness he dared to forgive sins as only God could do.

And yet Jesus entered our sinful world and consented in his humanity to submit to the human struggle so as to allow the Father to be supreme in his life in every choice. He had to come to grips with himself as sheer gift of the Father, not to presume that the powers which he possessed could be used by him independently of the Father's will. The glimpse that the gospel accounts give us show Jesus in the desert temptations, in the Garden of Gethsemane and on the cross of Calvary, struggling as all of us must struggle in order to win the gift of freedom by total self-surrender to the Father.

Freedom for Jesus as for you is God's gift, but it is won by a great struggle wherein the isolated self surrenders to the true self in love, freely given. Even in the development of Jesus' human freedom, there could be no growth in freedom without conflict, nor could there be any true love as a free gift to the Father in the choices he made at each moment.

Jesus—A Whole Person   In a retreat there are so many aspects of the human Christ that could appeal to us. In years past we have contemplated the Jesus of the gospels. We have our favorite scenes that render Jesus most present and most human to us. There are also certain sermons or bits of conversations of Jesus that hold us in intimacy with the heart that uttered those words and still utters them within our heart. Perhaps the best way to contemplate him today is to let those favorite scenes or passages come to us around the theme of Jesus, free to be a whole person.

Jesus is given to us that all human beings may become integrated as he was. The great work of Jesus is that through his death and resurrection he may live within us and pour out his Spirit, who can bring us with our cooperation into human wholeness. By contemplating Jesus as a whole person we can be drawn to the goal of our human existence. We can be attracted to him who is all-powerful to effect such integration in our lives.

What should strike us from the pages of the gospels is that Jesus responds to each situation with a balance and moderation that avoid any excess. Without losing a human richness and warmth that always attract others to him, Jesus can be alone with his heavenly Father in deep prayer, seemingly wanting to avoid the society of human beings. Yet we find him completely at home as he preaches and ministers in all kinds of self-sacrificing situations. He could be very gentle and filled with compassion and mercy; yet he could show himself strong and even angry toward hypocrites who made a mockery of serving God.

He adapts wonderfully to each situation because he seeks always the loving presence of his Father in every event. The Father is the guide and master and Jesus seeks only to act and react insofar as he can glorify the Father. He is freed from self-absorption as he responds with the fullness of his being in the intense consciousness of, not only knowing his true identity as the Son of the heavenly Father, but of becoming that loving Son in his joyful response of living each moment according to the good pleasure of his Father.

He came to fulfill the Law, not to destroy it. Still he swung free of any legalism as the Spirit of the Father breathed true life into the traditions that Jesus inherited from his Jewish religion. He was free of the opinions of other men as he strove to please only his Father. He was free of all inordinate human attachments so that he could love each man and woman whom he met with the same unique Spirit of love that the Father possessed.

In Jesus, body, soul and spirit relationships blended into one harmonious personality of great richness and delicate nuance that continued to grow as he accepted each moment as a challenge to *become* even more the realized person he was

97

being called to be. He is your model of how to become free by showing you how he lived each moment at the deepest level of his unique "I," the perfect image of his Father. At that center he consciously felt himself coming from the Father's free love and in that gift he freely sought to return himself as total gift to the Father.

Meditation

St. Paul writes: "When Christ freed us, he meant us to remain free" (Ga 5:1). Spend some time today contemplating the beautifully integrated personality of Jesus as he developed into greater becoming by acting freely at each moment. See some of the diverse situations in which he found himself and how he reacted with the fullness of his being as rooted in intense consciousness of the indwelling presence of the Father, always assuring him of his identity in infinite love.

Place yourself beside him and see what level of harmonious integration you have attained as shown by your daily actions and reactions to the different events that make up your life and give you the call to *become* more free and more completely the human person that God intends you to be. Jesus is continually releasing his Spirit within you to lead you into an abiding experience of God's love for you in Christ Jesus. That Spirit alone can free you from your unreal self and bring you into the true liberty of your real personhood that finds its completeness in loving surrender at all times to God the Father in union with Jesus. "Where the Spirit of the Lord is, there is freedom" (2 Cor 3:17).

Pray earnestly that the Spirit who brought Jesus ever-increasing levels of freedom will lead you into a similar freedom. Let St. Paul's words become your plan of life:

> If you are led by the Spirit, no law can touch you. When self-indulgence is at work the results are obvious. . . . What the Spirit brings is very different: love, joy, peace, patience,

kindness, goodness, trustfulness, gentleness and self-control. There can be no law against things like that, of course. You cannot belong to Christ Jesus unless you crucify all self-indulgent passions and desires. Since the Spirit is our life, let us be directed by the Spirit (Ga 5:16-25).

II: *The Gentle Jesus*

By now you have found your second wind. You are able to listen to God with a gentle spirit. You are actively receptive to the movements of God's Spirit. Now you are ready to contemplate Jesus in all his gentle openness to his Father's Spirit. Pray that the wholeness of Jesus' personality may become a model of your growing integration.

We Westerners have great need of gentleness to complement our rather one-sided character of aggressiveness. We receive our identity so often by what we do or possess, by whom we know among the powerful and wealthy. To speak of gentleness so often brings to our mind the image of softness and lack of character.

Is it not strange how we select elements from the Old and New Testaments to create God according to our own image? The Jews of the time of Christ had fashioned an image of God who was to be an aggressive restorer of their lost power. He was a terrifying, even cruel, vindictive God who demanded absolute obedience to each "jot and tittle" of the Law.

Jesus came as the gentle Lamb of God to restore to the human race the correct image of the heavenly Father.

Yet how many different images of Jesus do various Christians present, again so often according to their own value system? Some see Jesus as the liberal reformer of all of society's ills. In a Jansenistic view Jesus is seen as the stern lawgiver who remains totally removed from this material world and demands that his disciples also have nothing to do with it. Others create the "pietistic" Jesus who is saccharine and plastic and answers all one's selfish needs without a view toward healthy self-giving to others.

What is your habitual image of Jesus? Contemplate from the pages of the gospel the whole Jesus in all of his integrated personality. He came on this earth to show us the Father: "To have seen me is to have seen the Father" (Jn 14:9). But he also came to win our love and devotion in order that we could freely surrender to his divinizing Spirit. St. Irenaeus of the second century writes:

> For this is why the Word of God is man, and this is why the Son of God became the Son of Man, that man might possess the Word, receive adoption and become the son of God.

He came to show you what you should be, for you have been created by God according to his likeness. He wishes to release his Spirit in order that you might attain the fullness of your true self in him. You will attain integration of your true self in him when you become gentle to his operations within your life. See Jesus from the pages of the New Testament as gentle and find there the secret of your integration into a fully developed human being as he was.

A Gentle Spirit   The gentleness of Jesus was his way of existing in the truth of his Father's awesome transcendence. The Father was greater than he and without the Father the Son could do nothing (Jn 5:30; 14:28). Everything Jesus had, by way of revealed word or power of healing and miracles, came to him from the Father (Jn 5:20). The Father was always working (Jn 5:17) and Jesus gently worked together with him. He was not an automaton without free will, but in all things he turned inward to find his Father at the center of his being (Jn 14:11). There in the depths of his heart, his innermost consciousness, Jesus touched the Holy. He breathed, smiled, laughed and wept in that holy presence of his infinitely loving Father. All outside creatures, touching Jesus in new, surprising experiences, were received as gifts by that delicate, sensitive gentleness in him. Absent were the moods of aggressive autonomy and uncontrolled self-indulgence. Jesus was always present to the Father because the Father was always speaking his loving word in him.

Jesus constantly was wrapt in the loving presence of his Father who poured his Spirit of love into Jesus' being. With joyful response Jesus delighted to love his Father in each person encountered by Jesus. He discovered in the matrix of each event the material to be received gently and transformed into love returned.

A Flaming Presence of Love   From the pages of the New Testament notice how often you find references to nature, to the inanimate and the plant and animal worlds around Jesus. He was sensitive to the presence of his Father in all creatures. Lambs freshly born, seeds sown in the soft earth, the rain and its cleansing power, the birds that never stored grain into barns, the fox in its den, the grape vines being pruned, the flaming sunset, spangling the west with portents of fair weather, all creatures shouted out to the gentle Jesus that his Father was near, holy, beautiful, good and loving. And Jesus too wanted to be gentle and loving as his Father was.

Children have an ability to detect when a person is truly gentle and loving. How they must have experienced the gentleness of Jesus in a very deep way as he put his arms around them and blessed them:

> People were bringing little children to him for him to touch them. The disciples turned them away, but when Jesus saw this he was indignant and said to them, "Let the little children come to me; do not stop them; for it is to such as these that the kingdom of God belongs. I tell you solemnly,

101

anyone who does not welcome the kingdom of God like a little child will never enter it." Then he put his arms around them, laid his hands on them and gave them his blessing (Mk 10:13-16).

How gentle Jesus was toward people broken in body, soul and spirit! He came to die for love of the whole world, but he never refused to heal any human being, maimed or sick, so great was his compassion for the sheep scattered without a shepherd. We see his gentle thoughtfulness toward the widow of Naim:

> When the Lord saw her he felt sorry for her. "Do not cry," he said. Then he went up and put his hand on the bier . . . and said, "Young man, I tell you to get up." . . . and Jesus gave him to his mother (Lk 7:13-16).

He had pity on the multitudes in the desert who followed to hear his word and had nothing to eat so he fed them by multiplying the loaves and the fishes (Mk 6:34-44; 8:1-10). He wept over the hardness of the people of Jerusalem:

> Jerusalem, Jerusalem, you that kill the prophets and stone those who are sent to you! How often have I longed to gather your children, as a hen gathers her chicks under her wings, and you refused! (Mt 23:37-38).

Heart Speaks to Heart   The greatest gentleness of the heart of Christ is shown in his openness to receiving the beauty of his Father in the gifts of other human beings, beginning with his beautiful mother, Mary. Children receive many traits from their parents. Is it too far-fetched to think that Jesus first saw how a human being is gentle by watching his mother move through his life with complete freedom and gentleness of spirit? She was always interiorly saying: "I am the handmaid of the Lord . . . let what you have said be done to me" (Lk 1:38). Sensitive, totally feminine, Mary was open to the needs of her son, Jesus, and her husband, Joseph, of her neighbors and relatives and all whom she met.

How gentle Jesus is in his strong, virile love for Peter, a love so different from the love he gave to John and James and Judas! At the Last Supper Jesus allowed John the Beloved to place his head affectionately close to his breast. This same John could write that he and the other disciples had not only seen the Word who is life but they also had touched him (1 Jn 1:1). Jesus truly loved Lazarus as a friend over whose death he could weep tears of deep affection and sadness: "Jesus wept; and the Jews said, 'See how much he loved him!'" (Jn 11:37).

With special gentleness Jesus gave his love to the women who came into his life, and he revealed the tenderness of his Father's love as he not only gave them his love but gently received their love in return. Women traveled with Jesus to serve him, especially some like Mary Magdalene from whom he drove seven demons and Joanna, the wife of Herod's steward, Chuza, Susanna and "several others who provided for them out of their own resources" (Lk 8:2-3). Mary Magdalene, a prostitute, was touched by Jesus in his gentleness as no man had ever touched her before. She is found standing beside the gentle virgin-mother Mary at the foot of the cross. Her passionate love for him found her with a wild desire to take the body of Jesus away. But the gentle Jesus dispelled this with one simple word, "Mary!" (Jn 20:16). No human being ever pronounced her name as did the risen Jesus, for no human person knew her and loved her in her heavenly Father's love as did the gentle Jesus.

A Strong Gentleness   Far from being a weakling in his gentleness, Jesus shows on many pages of the New Testament that his very gentle spirit, open to the Father's guiding Spirit, would flare out from time to time in just anger and reproof. The Father had given him all rights to judge (Jn 5:22). He had "appointed him supreme judge" (Jn 5:27).

He slashed out against the hypocrisy of the religious leaders of his time (Lk 11:37-40; Jn 5:37-47; Mt 12:24-25, 31-34). The whole 23rd chapter of Matthew's gospel is a powerful indictment of the teaching classes of the Jews by a very "angry" Jesus. He called them "Hypocrites!" "Whitewashed tombs!" "Serpents, brood of vipers!" Jesus was hardly a lily-livered milquetoast! Like his Father, he was a "consuming fire" (Heb 12:29).

He entered into the sacred Temple where his Father, and only he was to be adored, but he saw merchants and moneychangers transform it into a den of thieves. With zeal for his Father's glory, he overturned their tables and drove the merchants and moneychangers out of the Temple. Still, for those who drove his hands and feet into the wood of the cross he could only gently ask his heavenly Father to forgive them, for they really did not understand what they were doing (Lk 23:34).

Upon Peter, his very specially chosen disciple who was meant to strengthen his brother disciples, Jesus could turn and reprove him severely for his worldliness in refusing Jesus the cross since Peter did not have much affection for suffering: "Get behind me, Satan! You are an obstacle in my path, because the way you think is not God's way but man's" (Mt 16:23). This same Peter, who with mock bravado was ready to go to prison and die with Jesus but who in fact betrayed his Master three times, received the gentle forgiveness of Jesus.

Before the Father's Face   Jesus was consistently gentle because he was at one with the loving Father. He knew his identity in the flaming love that the Father poured into his heart. He did not have to study other human beings in order to know how to act and react with gentleness in all human situations that confronted him. He needed only to turn within himself and in the depths of his being he found his Father, bathing him with his uncreated energies of love. His nature was to be gentle because that was the nature of his Father. Jesus could call out to us to learn of him "for I am gentle and humble in heart" (Mt 11:29).

In that contemplative, worshipful attitude, Jesus always lived and surrendered himself to his Father. Everything he did was done according to his will, and harmony in his person was the result. Isaiah could prophesy of the coming Messiah:

> . . . on him the spirit of Yahweh rests,
> a spirit of wisdom and insight,
> a spirit of counsel and power,
> a spirit of knowledge and of the fear of Yahweh. . . .
> He does not judge by appearances,
> he gives no verdict on hearsay,
> but judges the wretched with integrity,
> and with equity gives a verdict for the poor of the land.
> His word is a rod that strikes the ruthless,
> his sentences bring death to the wicked.
> Integrity is the loincloth round his waist,
> faithfulness the belt about his hips (Is 11:2-5).

Jesus, your king, comes to bring you into the kingdom of God. And the sign of that kingdom come among us is the gentleness of the lamb before its shearers (Is 53:7). The gentle Jesus pours out his Spirit of love into your heart to break down the power structures and the aggressive attacks whereby you seek to maintain your unreal self, and to allow you to surrender in a gentle spirit to his Father and to your neighbor in self-sacrificing love. He leads you to a heart knowledge that he and the Father are one in their gentle readiness to be vulnerable and to suffer as they wait for your return of love.

Realizing that God is a trinity of loving persons living

within you and loving you with a gentleness of suffering love made manifest through the crucified Jesus, you now can also afford to be gentle. Your strength, like that of God and Jesus, lies in your gentle love that is enduring and accepts all things.

> Love is always patient and kind; it is never jealous; love is never boastful or conceited; it is never rude or selfish; it does not take offence, and is not resentful. Love takes no pleasure in other people's sins but delights in the truth; it is always ready to excuse, to trust, to hope, and to endure whatever comes (1 Cor 13:4-7).

Such a gentle love of God poured into your heart will drive out all fear (1 Jn 4:18). Your values of true power and true, human worth are measured by the power of the gentle Jesus working in your life: "God's weakness is stronger than human strength" (1 Cor 1:25). Your true strength will begin to consist in a well-rounded personality, capable of freely giving love to all who enter into your life. This is the secret power of Christianity: to lose your unreal self and, through a gentle spirit receiving the Spirit of Jesus crucified and risen, to find your true self in a whole, human being that is growing in each moment according to the likeness of the gentle Jesus.

Meditation

Prayerfully reflect on the various images from the gospels (Mk 10:13-16) that these words of St. Tychon of Zadonsk, the Russian saint of the 18th century, beautifully capture:

> Listen, my soul: God has come to us;
> Our Lord has visited us.
> For my sake He was born of the Virgin Mary,
> He was wrapped in swaddling clothes,
> He who covers heaven with the clouds
> and vests Himself with robes of light.
> For my sake He was placed in the lowly manger,

He whose throne is the heavens and whose feet rest upon
    earth.
For my sake He was fed with His mother's milk,
He who feeds all creatures.
For my sake He was held in His mother's arms,
He who is borne by the Cherubim
and holds all creatures in His embrace.
For my sake He was circumcised according to the law,
He who is maker of the Law.
For my sake, He who is unseen
became visible and lived among men,
He who is my God.
My God became one like me, like a man;
the word became flesh,
and my Lord, the Lord of Glory,
took for my sake the form of a servant
and lived upon earth and walked upon earth
He who is the King of Heaven.
He labored, worked miracles,
conversed with men, was like a servant,
He who is the Lord of all.
He was hungry and thirsty,
He who provides food and drink for all creatures.
He wept, He who wipes away all tears.
He suffered and mourned,
He who is the consoler of all men.
He consorted with sinners,
He who alone is just and holy.
He who is omnipotent toiled
and had nowhere to lay His head,
He who lives in light inaccessible.
He was poor,
He who gives riches to all men.
He wandered from town to town and from place to place,
He who is omnipresent and fills all space.
And thus for thirty-three years and more
He lived and labored upon earth for my sake—
I who am His servant.

107

III: *Need for Discipline*

Jesus healed the sick and stretched out his almighty hands and called to all who labored and were heavily burdened to come to him and he would refresh them (Mt 11:28). He fed the crowds miraculously with bread and they wanted to make him their king so that they would never want for any temporal good. His very disciples wanted to have the first places of honor beside him, pushing each other out of the way in their desire for superiority, but Jesus offered them only the cup of suffering. How clearly Jesus demonstrated this to Peter after he foretold his future sufferings, death and resurrection:

> From that time Jesus began to make it clear to his disciples that he was destined to go to Jerusalem and suffer grievously at the hands of the elders and chief priests and scribes, to be put to death and to be raised up on the third day. Then, taking him aside, Peter started to remonstrate with him. "Heaven preserve you, Lord," he said, "this must not happen to you." But he turned and said to Peter, "Get behind me, Satan! You are an obstacle in my path, because the way you think is not God's way but man's" (Mt 16:21-23).

The rich young man wanted to follow Christ but when Jesus asked him to sell whatever he owned and to give the money to the poor and then follow him, the young man turned away sad, "for he was a man of great wealth" (Mt 19:22).

Whenever Jesus told his would-be followers that if they wanted to have a part with him they would have to deny themselves, take up the cross and follow him, his followers became fewer. Many Christians down through the centuries have begun to follow Jesus but have turned away from greater union with him and perfection in the Christian life of love and humble service toward others because they were not ready to shoulder the cross of self-abnegation.

108

Paradox of True Life   Jesus preached a doctrine that contained many paradoxes, but the greatest is summarized in the saying: "Anyone who finds his life will lose it; anyone who loses his life for my sake will find it" (Mt 10:39). His other statement reinforces the former: "Unless a wheat falls on the ground and dies, it remains only a single grain; but if it dies, it yields a rich harvest. Anyone who loves his life loses it" (Jn 12:24-25). Just as Jesus preached his doctrine, so he lived it. The terrible carrying of his cross to Calvary, his mounting it to preach with his dying gasp the saving doctrine of dying to self, only to bear fruit in the resurrection, is a summary of what every Christian's life should be. This principle of death-resurrection is at work in all of nature. Nothing lives but that something must die; nothing dies but that something new lives. In our spiritual life, there must be a constant dying to those elements that prevent our full growth, so that God may live completely in us. Jesus is affirming that if we wish to live in union with him and his Father and be what we should be, loving children of God, bringing forth the fruit of the Holy Spirit (Ga 5:22), we must die to everything that is an impediment to letting God have complete dominance in our lives. This is also necessary if we are to fulfill the great commandments, to love not only God with our whole heart, mind and strength, but also to love our neighbor (Mt 22:37-40).

The goal of our Christian life is to be loving toward God and also toward others. Life is to be apostolic, to bring forth the fruit of love in building up a loving community, the body of Christ, the church. Jesus said: "I commissioned you to go out and bear fruit, fruit that will last" (Jn 15:16). But we realize that there can be no fruit produced unless we remain in Christ: "Whoever remains in me, with me in him, bears fruit in plenty" (Jn 15:5). Separated from Christ there can be no true fruit of Christian love shown to God or neighbor.

Guarding Your Heart   Jesus taught that we are to guard our heart, for within us is the motivating power to decide whether we act out of self-sacrificing love or out of self-centeredness: "But the things that come out of the mouth come from the heart, and it is these that make a man unclean" (Mt 15:18-20). The great masters of the spiritual life, starting with St. Paul, have always taught the necessity of what Cassian called "purity of heart." This is a loving attention and vigilance over every thought and movement of our "heart," the Semitic or scriptural way of referring to the deepest layers of our consciousness and even the unconscious.

Teilhard de Chardin called it "passionate indifference," a sensitive turning to God who dwells within us, to determine whether this or that thought is really in harmony with the Father's will. It is a mental sobriety, a balance, an internal disposition of attention to the movement of God's Spirit leading us to true discernment as to how we should act and react to any given situation or temptation according to our true dignity as God's loving children.

Through such inner discipline and recollection before the Lord, we are no longer moved impulsively by our own desires and passions, but we hold ourselves in abeyance until we know how this or that thought relates to the mind of God. God is the living criterion of our choices, but what an inner discipline and inner knowledge of the movements of our heart this demands on our part!

Know Thyself   St. Peter writes: "Be calm but vigilant, because your enemy the devil is prowling round like a roaring lion, looking for someone to eat. Stand up to him, strong in faith" (1 P 5:8). It is not only fallen angels who can attack us but it is also those hidden areas of darkness and brokenness that prevent us from responding fully to God's presence at each moment of our life. St. Augustine in the 10th book of his *Confessions* describes these hidden and repressed areas in these words:

> . . . for there are in me those lamentable darknesses I know so well and in the midst of them the powers of my own soul that in me lie hidden from me. The result is that when my mind of its own strength puts questions to itself it does not feel that it can readily credit the answers that it gets.

The ascetical life begins with knowing the dark side of ourselves, the negative elements that are obstacles to our communion with God. This centers not only on our knowledge of such "entanglements" with the things of the "flesh," but also on our vigorous and constant effort to root out such attachments on the body, soul and spirit levels. The ascetical life embraces all of our efforts both in prayer and in actual living situations to put on the mind of Christ and live the Christian virtues that flow from the "old man" becoming now the "new man" in Christ. Such Christian virtues all lead to the main virtue that embraces all others, namely, that of charity (1 Cor 13:13).

Reflective Healing   Knowledge of the dark side of our consciousness and unconscious is not enough; true self-knowledge demands that such areas of brokenness, once discovered, should be brought under the healing power of Jesus Christ in prayerful reflection. The more you can reflect under the power of the Holy Spirit, even daily before going to sleep, upon your daily activities and bring the hurts and even the victories under the affirmation of Jesus the Lord, the more you will gain inner healing and move to a new level of your true identity in God's great love for you, as you identify now with the "real" self that you are becoming in Christ.

One of the traditional, ascetical practices found in all ages of Christianity is that of the examination of conscience. This must be more than an exercise to discover what sins you have committed. It should accentuate the present, freeing, healing power of God's Word, Jesus Christ, to heal you as you see your concrete brokenness. This exercise has five phases: 1) Thanksgiving and praise to God for all the gifts of a given day; 2) petition to the Spirit of Jesus to enlighten you to see yourself as God sees you, in accord with the living word of God; 3) a review in the presence of God of the present day: seeing the positive elements of your cooperation; seeing how you may have failed in thought, word and deed; seeing the areas of omission in not corresponding to God's delicate inspirations of grace; 4) crying out for the healing power of Jesus Christ to come upon you and heal any brokenness, to forgive you anything that was a transgression against God's holy will, especially in the area of love toward others (see Jesus stretching out his healing hands upon this or that area, this or that relationship and bringing to it a wholeness); 5) a quick look at the next day with a humble prayer to beg God's presence and power of love to live that day as fully as possible according to his love and grace.

The Problem of Asceticism   Too long Christian teaching on the ascetical life has been based on a non-Christian view of the human person. Through such influences as Platonism, Manichaeism, Stoicism and early Christian monasticism that taught an unhealthy withdrawal from the material world and an exaggerated separation of body and soul as distinct parts making up the human person, Christians have sought to beat down the body as an enemy to the soul. We need a more biblical understanding of our human nature which shows that the whole person is made "according to the image and likeness" of God (Gn 1:26), and that includes the human body. We are not sinful by our human nature but by the *sarx* in us which means that "flesh" element in us which through the sin of the world makes us tend toward self-centeredness rather than toward self-sacrificing love. We are torn between our "carnal mind" and that of the spirit within us.

Jesus has entered into our estrangement, becoming like us in all his temptations, save sin (Heb 4:15). He condemned sin in the flesh by dying on the cross and through his resurrection he pours out his Spirit to lead us away from sin and death into a sharing in his risen life that is proved by our love for God and one another.

Jesus the Ascetic   Jesus shows in his human life that his whole being had to be brought under the discipline of love for his heavenly Father. It was not his own will that he came to do but to seek always to do that of his Father (Lk 22:43). Whatever he did by way of external and internal discipline was a means, in order that he could be free to express most perfectly the return of love to the Father for the infinite love that he had received from him. "Christ did not think of himself" (Rm 15:3) writes St. Paul. He sought always to please his Father (Jn 8:29).

His self-denial was always a sign of his wholehearted devotedness to God. Jesus had the physical appetites for food, drink and sex that all of us have. He had emotions that had to be subordinated to the pleasure and the glory of his Father. He had to hone his intellect and will to become perfect instruments so that he as a whole person was always turned in loving surrender to the Father. Thus his asceticism consisted in an attitude of faith that embraced any act of self-denial that would positively allow him to unite himself more totally with the Father.

Jesus taught this doctrine because he lived it throughout his entire human life: "If your eye is sound, your whole body will be filled with light" (Mt 6:22). It is the seed falling into the ground and dying in order to bear much fruit

(Jn 12:24). The cross was not a negative attitude toward life but a positive freeing of Jesus to live completely for the Father.

In such a perspective Jesus did not do merely what he felt he had to do, the minimum, in order to keep himself from sin. As he continued daily in prayer to experience the infinite love of God for him, he was moved in his controlled living that came always under the commands and expressed wishes of his Father to go even further. He wanted to invent spontaneous expressions of his desire to give himself completely into the hands of the Father. "He who sent me is with me, and has not left me to myself, for I always do what pleases him" (Jn 8:29). This is where his human freedom and love reach their peak and asceticism moves into mystical union with the one loved.

Deny Yourself   Some persons seek to return their love to God by a minimum performance of what they see as commands which they *have* to obey in order to keep from committing mortal sins. Others go much further in their desire to obey God's wishes and refrain from any deliberate turning away from him. But when you have deeply experienced the love of God as expressed in the *kenosis* of Jesus poured out completely on the cross for love of you, then you freely want at every moment to create ways of "incarnating" or putting flesh to your love. For, unless that love finds concrete expression in acts freely chosen, it will remain always inside of you and be suffocated for lack of generous self-giving.

> Jesus said:
> "The Father loves me
> because I lay down my life
> in order to take it up again.
> No one takes it from me;
> I lay it down of my own free will,
> and as it is in my power to lay it down,
> so it is in my power to take it up again" (Jn 10:17-18).

114

God at this stage of your retreat is moving on two levels in your prayer. Through the pages of the New Testament he is revealing to you his perfect love as expressed in Jesus, his Son, especially as he enters into his total self-emptying on the cross. On the other hand, his Spirit is stirring you to the very natural response to such love given: "What shall I return to God for all the love he has given to me?" How generous have you been in your return of yourself as gift to God? What compromises have you made in your attachments to persons, things, places, work?

Your ascetical control over all your faculties of body, soul and spirit is the measure of your return of love to God. Asceticism is truly an ongoing process of freeing your self so as to live dynamically according to the full potential which God has placed within you. Discipline and moderation, moving at times into creative suffering that may seem to the outsider an excessive and "unnecessary" death to self, will be your index of how seriously in love you are with God. It is something the Spirit moves you to as a symbol of the love welling up within you toward the God who has given you all in Christ.

Your efforts along the lines of ascetical discipline can never bring forth the fruit of the Father (Jn 15:4), that is, his shared life lived by you as a child of God. But such efforts are the emptying that disposes you to allow the full power of the Spirit to accomplish his work in you, the work of divinizing you according to the image and likeness of Jesus.

Meditation

Place yourself before Jesus as he stands before Pilate. *Ecce homo!* Behold the man! See him in all his emptiness, ready to give you his whole being. Here is your king and Lord who is asking you not for compromises but for total gift in return. "Was it not ordained that the Christ should suffer and so enter into his glory?" (Lk 24:26). Is there any other

115

way than the cross of self-denial, going against your false self, so that you also may enter into the glory and the sharing in the risen life of Jesus Christ?

> I have been crucified with Christ, and I live now not with my own life but with the life of Christ who lives in me. The life I now live in this body I live in faith: faith in the Son of God who loved me and who sacrificed himself for my sake (Ga 2:19-20).

Jesus, Broken Love

We have seen earlier that God has called us to be his chosen, loving children — to be holy. St. Paul summarizes God's plan when he writes:

> Before the world was made, he chose us, chose us in Christ,
> to be holy and spotless, and to live through love in his presence,
> determining that we should become his adopted sons, through Jesus Christ
> for his own kind purposes,
> to make us praise the glory of his grace,
> his free gift to us in the Beloved (Ep 1:4-6).

What has holiness meant for you? When we examine God's holiness in scripture we see God as relational to men and angels, moving toward them as gift, to share his own trinitarian life with them. God's holiness is God offering himself in loving, self-giving relationships with us in order that we may share most intimately in his very own nature (2 P 1:4).

God calls us to receive his holiness of self-giving and to become holy by the gift of ourselves to all that we meet and serve: "Be holy in all you do, since it is the Holy One who has called you, and scripture says: Be holy, for I am holy" (1 P 1:15-16).

You are called to be a saint, a holy person, sanctified by God's holiness (Rm 1:7; 1 Cor 1:2). But his holiness cannot be experienced except through his image, Jesus Christ, who offers us the total gift of himself. But what a strange idea many Christians have of the holiness of Jesus! His holiness is too often seen as static since he is by nature divine. We so often fail to realize that he was also fully human as we are.

Jesus became holy through the struggle that was constantly his to surrender himself completely to the dominance of his heavenly Father. It was in the interior battle that Jesus had to become holy by imaging the self-giving of his Father toward us in perfect humility. Jesus became sinless as he yielded to God's Spirit within him and went against any urge toward independence away from the will of the Father.

I: *Jesus Tempted*

Jesus was driven into the desert by the Holy Spirit (Mk 1:12) and there he was tempted. We read of various temptations to which Jesus was subjected during his public ministry (Mk 8:11, 27-33; 10:35-40; Jn 2:18-19; 6:15, 30-31; 7:1-9; 12:12-18). But the synoptic writers give special significance to the three desert temptations because they are a model of what Jesus underwent in his struggle all his lifetime. Biblical exegetes have made many attempts to explain the desert temptations. What is essential is that Jesus had to struggle within his heart to reach the state of loving surrender to the Father.

In the first temptation, St. Matthew's gospel tells us that Jesus was driven into the wilderness by the Spirit "to be tempted by the devil" (Mt 4:1-4). After 40 days and nights of fasting and praying, Jesus was very hungry. The tempter sought to induce Jesus, if he really was the Son of God, to turn stones into bread and feed himself. What seems to be the essence of this temptation, which could have been repeated all through Jesus' human life, was the attraction to use his messianic powers to satisfy basic, human needs and not to trust in his heavenly Father to provide for them in more ordinary ways.

Jesus not only taught trust, but he strove always to live in a state of complete reliance on the Father's providential care: "Do not worry; do not say, 'What are we to eat? What are we to drink?' . . . Your heavenly Father knows you need them all. Set your hearts on his kingdom first, and on his righteousness, and all these other things will be given you as well" (Mt 6:31-33; Lk 12:29-31). And now he was tempted to take charge over his life instead of submitting himself totally to the care of the Father. He repulsed the temptation as a misuse of his messianic powers that were to be signs announcing that the kingdom of God was breaking in upon his listeners.

Here in the desert Jesus would not use the powers given him to lead others to the Father by insisting on his prerogatives as the Son of God. If he had the power, the temptation went, why should he not use it to remove some temporary unpleasantness such as hunger and thirst? Jesus repels the devil by quoting from Deuteronomy 8:3: "Man does not live on bread alone but . . . on every thing that comes from the mouth of Yahweh."

Here we see the humility of Jesus; like a released arrow, he goes right to the target of his whole dedication, the Father. He is the word that by nature reflects always the divine mind of the Father who speaks that word. He knows that all he has is from the Father and now and always he should seek to correspond to the Father's wishes. His magnificent obsession is always to serve the Father and to do nothing or even to wish nothing but what the Father wishes. He rejects the temptation to act independently of the Father. And because he strives always to be obedient to the Father, he brings joy to the Father: "This is my Son, the Beloved; my favor rests on him" (Mt 3:17).

Temptation to Presumption   In the second temptation of
Jesus we see again that the basic movement of sin is in the
human desire to act independently of God. Jesus is described in this temptation as being enticed to presume that
the Father would come to his rescue if Jesus were to put
himself in a situation that would demand a test of the
Father's love for him.

> The devil then took him to the holy city and made him stand
> on the parapet of the Temple. "If you are the Son of God" he
> said, "throw yourself down; for scripture says: He will put
> you in his angels' charge, and they will support you on their
> hands in case you hurt your foot against a stone" (Mt 4:5-6).

Jesus must have often found himself in a position in
which he was tempted either to prove to himself or to others
around him that he was powerful and really the Son of God.
In his humanity he was growing always into this experience
by humble obedience to the will of his Father. But this second temptation describes all those situations in which Jesus
was tempted to presume that he could force the Father's
hand and have his dignity saved by power and not by
humility.

The demonic around and within Jesus, the potential to
say *yes* or *no* to his heavenly Father, set up situations
throughout his life in which he could grow into his true identity. Now in the desert the devil tempted Jesus to do
something to prove that he was the Son of God: If you really
are the Son of God, the Father would certainly have to protect you in any and all situations, no matter how bizarre.
You, after all, have a right to demand this type of love and
submission from your Father. All you have to do is to throw
yourself off the Temple parapet and the Father will immediately send his angels to protect you: "If you are the Son
of God . . ." But Jesus humbly bows his head and whispers,
"Yes, Father." He rejects independent power, pride and
presumption by obedience, poverty of spirit and humility.

Jesus responds by quoting Deuteronomy 6:16: "You must not put the Lord your God to the test" (Mt 4:7). He had not come to this earth to tempt God but to submit in loving obedience to his will. His whole essence as Son was to be total gift back to the Father from whom he had received everything. He was not greater than the Father. Therefore Jesus would not tempt the Father to insist on his own power to perform signs and wonders in order to win the acclaim of the world. He would win only the good pleasure of his Father through humility. His true power as the imaged Son of the Father would be his weakness to submit in love at all times to the Father. He would conquer worldly power by loving obedience and that even unto death.

Worldly Possessions   In the third temptation Jesus is presented by the evil ruler of the kingdom of darkness with a view of worldly riches, honors and power.

> Next, taking him to a very high mountain, the devil showed him all the kingdoms of the world and their splendor. "I will give you all these," he said, "if you fall at my feet and worship me." Then Jesus replied, "Be off, Satan! For scripture says:
> You must worship the Lord your God,
> and serve him alone" (Mt 4:8-10).

All human beings, and Jesus is no exception, are constantly tempted to attain their identity through possessing things that indicate power. Riches, honors, accomplishments, these signs of power are what Jesus and all human beings are tempted to seek. But Jesus resists such a temptation by living out the scriptural text that he quotes from Deuteronomy 6:13: Only God is worthy of worship and obedient service and in him alone and not in things of power would he seek his identity. Jesus lived out all his life what he himself had taught: You cannot serve two masters. It must be either God or Mammon.

121

The kingdom of God is not of this world (Jn 18:36). God's kingdom is characterized by poverty of spirit. Jesus, by living such poverty of spirit, would conquer the worldly kingdom and give power to his followers to live as he did in this creation of God's kingdom. Jesus lived poorly. Possessions did not possess him; he swung freely from any inordinate attachment to use such gifts from God as though they were ends in themselves or he were the end of his own existence.

> Remember how generous the Lord Jesus was: he was rich, but he became poor for your sake, to make you rich out of his poverty (2 Cor 8:9).

Because Jesus was humble of heart and detached from power, he was able to love freely all persons who came into his life and thus he would grow into the human expression of the Father's infinite love for all his children. Rooted in the self-sacrificing love that his Father poured into his heart, Jesus gave himself in a similar emptying love for all of us in loving service: "As the Father has loved me, so I have loved you" (Jn 15:9). He lived for love of the Father and of all human beings, not for himself.

Tempted As You   How easy it is to see yourself in the temptations that came to the human Jesus. Continually you are being tempted to use your God-given powers to overcome unpleasant situations, especially personal suffering. Your insecurity before God and others tempts you to collect riches, honors and the credit of a great name on this earth so that you can find your identity in such false values. The more you see your identity in such "things" instead of in the love of God and neighbor, the more you are driven to accumulate more signs of power.

Each person develops his or her own set of symbols for

what is important and what will create the sense of well-being. Often it is our society that dictates what possessions are the signs of "having arrived." Look over your past life and see what stratagem the prince of darkness has employed to push you to acquire things that you have considered important. Has it perhaps been your desire for a certain type of work and excellence in that work in order to attain power and honor? Has it been an attachment to a certain person who at least indirectly shapes your value system and your choices? Or has a place of residence been your attachment? Sometimes clothing, entertainment, an attachment to smoking, drinking, certain pleasures in food, can enslave us in a way that is not perhaps very radical and death-dealing to our devotion to God's holy will, but it deadens at least our fervor by throwing us off center.

Today would be a good time to study the pattern of your own set of predominant temptations to see how the demonic within you operates. Contrast that with the standard of Jesus who chooses in perfect obedience to the Father to live in obscurity, poverty, actual and in spirit, humble service and meekness toward all whom he has come to love and serve.

Meditation

Place yourself in the setting of the desert where Jesus went to be tempted. Watch him as he struggles to go deeper into his unconscious and bring everything within him under the dominance of his Father (Mt 4:1-11; Mk 1:12-13; Lk 4:1-13). Study your own interior pattern of temptations. What are the areas of weakness that take you away from the faithful following of Christ and his Spirit? Fill yourself with a burning desire to have a share in the values that led Jesus to a life of complete surrender in love to his Father and to the whole human race.

ALONE WITH THE ALONE

II: *The Suffering Servant*

No human being has ever escaped suffering during his or her earthly sojourn. The mystery of physical and moral evils that lies at the heart of so much human suffering will never be unraveled by human reasoning. Evil and its accompanying sufferings can be conquered only by faith, hope and love.

Look about you and see that the most pathetic and heart-rending suffering in human lives comes precisely in the context of human love. That which God meant to be an incarnation of his trinitarian self-giving, as two human beings give to each other the gift of themselves in an *I-thou* relationship moving toward a *we* community, so often becomes a living hell of self-estrangement or lonely isolation.

Death-Resurrection   God sent his Son into our world to reconcile us to him (Col 1:20). Jesus Christ came not to tell us the answer to the universal problem of evil, but to overcome evil, sin and death by his suffering love. Division and dissension, hatred and fear, aggressive power and exploitation could be conquered only by a gentle, suffering love unto death. By freely sacrificing his human life in dying for us, Jesus in his humanity was raised to glory by his Father's Spirit and is now able to live within us.

His self-giving unto death for love of us is God's plan to drive out fear in our lives: "Fear is driven out by perfect love" (1 Jn 4:18). Our human sufferings can be joyfully accepted and transformed into our return of love to him who is always present to us and always loving us unto death.

Jesus' answer to evil in the world is suffering love. He would have no power of Caesar or of this world. His power would be in his weakness and emptiness: "For God's foolishness is wiser than human wisdom, and God's weakness is stronger than human strength" (1 Cor 1:25). St.

Paul gives us an ancient Christian hymn that summarizes God's answer to evil:

> His state was divine,
> yet he did not cling
> to his equality with God
> but emptied himself
> to assume the condition of a slave,
> and became as men are,
> he was humbler yet,
> even to accepting death,
> death on a cross.
> But God raised him high
> and gave him the name
> which is above all other names
> so that all beings
> in the heavens, on earth and in the underworld,
> should bend the knee at the name of Jesus
> and that every tongue should acclaim
> Jesus Christ as Lord,
> to the glory of God the Father (Ph 2:6-11).

Obedient Unto Death   Jesus came to conquer evil by love. He came to serve his heavenly Father in humble obedience on our behalf. He knew in every choice, in every thought, word and deed, that he had come, not to do his own will, but to live in loving surrender to his heavenly Father. He lived only to please and bring him glory. He knew that everything he had came to him from his loving service: "Because I have come from heaven, not to do my own will, but to do the will of the one who sent me" (Jn 6:38).

Jesus lived in the loving presence of his Father. He constantly experienced his Father in the loving activities of daily life: "My Father goes on working, and so do I" (Jn 5:17). As the Father loved him (Jn 15:9) and served him in all things, so Jesus loves us and serves us.

That service to us, Jesus knew, would be a continued

self-forgetting that would climax in the free gift of himself on our behalf. He served the broken ones of this world. To any sick or disturbed person he brought comfort and healing. He touched the crowds with his words and his deep love for them. He forgave them their sins. He lived only to bring life and that more abundantly, to all who wanted it. He was totally available to all who needed him.

Suffering Servant   Jesus explained the role of the Messiah to the two disciples on the road to Emmaus:

> "You foolish men! So slow to believe the full message of the prophets! Was it not ordained that the Christ should suffer and so enter into his glory?" (Lk 24:25-26).

He had come to fulfill the prophets, especially Deutero-Isaiah, who had predicted that Yahweh's Messiah would be the Suffering Servant, "Ebed Yahweh."

> And yet ours were the sufferings he bore,
> ours the sorrows he carried.
> But we thought of him as someone punished,
> struck by God, and brought low.
> Yet he was pierced through for our faults,
> crushed for our sins.
> On him lies a punishment that brings us peace,
> And through his wounds we are healed (Is 53:4-5).

The Suffering Servant is not a victim of circumstances turned over to the wiles of men who persecute him. There is a plan of propitiation for the sins of mankind. He would bear the sins of the world and take them away, "letting himself be taken for a sinner, while he was bearing the faults of many and praying all the time for sinners" (Is 53:12). In his gentleness and meekness of heart he would become like a lamb that is led to the slaughterhouse, never opening its mouth before its shearers (Is 53:7).

All his lifetime Jesus willingly entered into human sufferings in order to become closer to us: "God dealt with sin by sending his own Son in a body as physical as any sinful body, and in that body God condemned sin" (Rm 8:3). In his humble service to people there was nothing to distinguish him from other persons. He was a hard-working carpenter. He knew hunger and thirst and fatigue. He grew in human knowledge, how to make things, cope with life's problems; above all, how to experience his Father's love in the love he gave to and received from the women and men who came into his life as his friends.

But he knew his great mission was to reach that level of human love that would image the immense love that the Father had for him and all of us. This would happen in "his hour" when on the cross the Suffering Servant of Yahweh would completely empty himself out in love. We understand something of the sufferings of Jesus through the poignant words of Deutero-Isaiah:

> Like a sapling he grew up in front of us,
> like a root in arid ground.
> Without beauty, without majesty (we saw him),
> no looks to attract our eyes;
> a thing despised and rejected by men,
> a man of sorrows and familiar with suffering,
> a man to make people screen their faces;
> he was despised and we took no account of him.
> And yet ours were the sufferings he bore,
> ours the sorrows he carried.
> But we, we thought of him as someone punished,
> struck by God; and brought low (Is 53:2-4).

Love Unto Death   The depths of Jesus' suffering, especially on the cross, can be understood only in terms of the infinite love he received in his human consciousness from his heavenly Father. Love begets love and suffering begets suffering. In the cross, on which he emptied himself totally out of love for the Father and for us, Jesus chose the most perfect sign of the infinite love of God for each one of us. Jesus on the cross was choosing to be in the human form of suffering what God is always like in his love for us.

When Jesus shrieked out in agonizing pain and darkest abandonment on the cross, "My God, my God, why have you deserted me?" (Mk 15:34), God's love for us was perfectly expressed. Jesus earlier had said: "The Father loves me because I lay down my life in order to take it up again. No one takes it from me; I lay it down of my own free will" (Jn 10:17-18). The Father loves Jesus because he, the Word of God, lays down his life freely in order to express definitively God's eternal love for mankind.

For You He Dies   St. Paul constantly realized that Jesus, the Son of God, sacrificed himself for his sake (Ga 2:20). This suffering servant, Jesus, is always loving you personally unto death. He lives within you and has that same, consuming love for you that he had on the cross. He is always leading you through his Spirit into the awesome presence of the heavenly Father as perfect holiness, beauty and love. You are now being loved by your infinitely loving Father through the service of Jesus, the Suffering Servant of Yahweh. Realizing this, you can be healed of your self-centeredness and be brought out of the entombment of your loneliness and inability to love others unto suffering. Jesus touches you and leads you into a transformation whereby you can now live no longer for yourself but you, too, with Jesus Christ can love others in suffering service.

> . . . and the reason he died for all was so that living men should live no longer for themselves, but for him who died and was raised to life for them (2 Cor 5:15).

To Live for Others   Christianity was meant to be practical. We are called to be Christians 24 hours of the day. As Jesus lived, so he exhorts us to live a life of self-sacrifice. Suffering has no meaning in itself. It is usually most dehumanizing when it is only suffering. But when suffering is part and parcel of expressing love for God and neighbor then suffering is beautiful and noble, even divine. If Jesus were the Suffering Servant, ought we not also at least want to have a share with him in such loving suffering for others?

If you truly wish to be the disciple of Jesus, you must embrace the cross of suffering out of love for others. Jesus makes great demands on those who wish to follow him; but that is only because love is always patient and kind and endures all things. Read the way Jesus wants his disciples to live and see how you line up with his requirements for his followers:

> ". . . bless those who curse you, pray for those who treat you badly. To the man who slaps you on one cheek, present the other cheek too; to the man who takes your cloak from you, do not refuse your tunic. Give to everyone who asks you and do not ask for your property back from the man who robs you. Treat others as you would like them to treat you. If you love those who love you, what thanks can you expect? Even sinners love those who love them. And if you do good to those who do good to you, what thanks can you expect? For even sinners do that much. And if you lend to those from whom you hope to receive, what thanks can you expect? Even sinners lend to sinners to get back the same amount. Instead, love your enemies and do good, and lend without any hope of return. . . . Give and there will be gifts for you; a full measure, pressed down, shaken together, and running over, will be poured into your lap; because the amount you measure out is the amount you will be given back" (Lk 6:28-38).

According to Jesus, you are to visit the sick, the lonely, the imprisoned, and give them love. They are all parts of his body and you are a part of them. How can you inflict harm upon anyone, even one who calls you an enemy? You must know in the love of God through the suffering of Jesus that you are a child of God and a brother or sister to every person created by God according to his image and likeness. Washing the feet of others is really washing your own feet and also washing the feet of the total Christ.

By showing love and humble service to all whom you meet, especially the most despised and "unlikeable" according to worldly standards, you become the sign of God's power to conquer evil and sin and death in your world. You make Jesus, the Suffering Servant, still walk among the sinful and broken ones, filled with evil and pain, and you allow him to bring again his healing love into their frightened hearts. You will find it difficult to suffer. But Jesus has suffered first and died to prove his love for you. Receive that suffering love and desire to become God's suffering love incarnated in your world. Pray, even though you do not feel much like praying, that you may share in the loving, suffering ministry of Jesus to the broken ones of this world.

Meditation

Prayerfully place yourself before Jesus and his disciples at the Last Supper. See how Jesus, the Suffering Servant of Yahweh, washes the feet of his disciples (Jn 13:2-16). "If I, then, the Lord and Master, have washed your feet, you should wash each other's feet. I have given you an example so that you may copy what I have done to you" (Jn 13:14-15). True love is always a suffering service to live for the other.

III: *Power to Love*

God has implanted in all human beings a drive to form loving communities. We come alive when we are with friends who love us and call us into new being. In loneliness we dry up and seemingly die. This is only to say that God is love and he has created us so that we may continually grow into greater oneness with the trinitarian community of Father, Son and Holy Spirit, as we learn to let go and love one another.

Death is so terrifying for us because we have an innate belief that our opportunities to grow in love on this earth have finally come to an end. A retreat is to enter in a way into a dying experience. We are led by God's Spirit deeply into ourselves, far beyond our habitual preconditioning thought-patterns and habits of doing things. We are asked to see ourselves in relationship to God and neighbor with an "ultimate concern," to quote Paul Tillich's phrase.

We begin to see that deep within us lies our real self crying out for fulfillment. An urgency comes over us to begin to live fully before it is too late! We have had throughout our life some experiences of living in the power of unselfish love for God and for others. We know the peace and joy, the meaningfulness that then came into our life. It was so right, the way it should be. We knew we were made for love, to live unselfishly for God and neighbor. We have known also how wrong it was when we withdrew from true love and lived only for self.

Meaningfulness   Scripture, as we have seen, describes that deep down "place" within us where we meet God and experience his infinite love for us as our *heart*. It really is not a place within our bodies, but it is the intensity of our conscious awareness whereby we can, as total persons, experience God as loving us and we can return ourselves freely as gift back to him. It is this *heart-experience* that gives us ultimate direction and meaning. Living in this rarefied atmosphere of unselfish love for God we move out of slavery into ever-increasing freedom.

The more we can live in God's love by finding him very close to us in every moment and in every activity, the more meaningfulness will come to our life. This loving God is not far removed from the monotony, the slow growth, even the apparent setbacks, the pains and the sufferings of our every day. He is "inside," present in his loving activities, seeking only to share himself more and more completely since that is the nature of free love.

God loves us, not because of what we can give him, but because he is so overflowing with exuberant richness that he wishes to share his very richness, his very self, as a trinitarian family, with us. He creates the entire world with so much richness and variety only for us human beings. He wishes to be present to us, communicating his infinite love for us in each created gift. Yet all such gifts are ways of bringing us to the realization that we really are children of God (1 Jn 3:1) as we recognize him as our loving Father, as indwelling gift, totally present to us in his Son and Spirit.

Our meaningfulness in life depends on how well we realize the truth that scripture reveals to us about our birth into the family of God.

> But to all who did accept him
> he gave power to become children of God,
> to all who believe in the name of him
> who was born not out of human stock
> or urge of the flesh
> or will of man
> but of God himself (Jn 1:12-13).

Your Response   What shall be your response to God's overwhelming love for you? It should be to live in unselfish love as you have experienced God living within your life. Jesus had experienced the infinite love of the Father for him and he in turn loves us infinitely. Our response should be then to love others as he has loved us. He teaches this so powerfully in his Last Supper discourse found in St. John's gospel, especially in chapter 15:

"As the Father has loved me,
so I have loved you.
Remain in my love,
If you keep my commandments
you will remain in my love
just as I have kept my Father's commandments
and remain in his love.
. . . This is my commandment:
love one another,
as I have loved you.
A man can have no greater love
than to lay down his life for his friends.
. . . What I command you
is to love one another" (Jn 15:9-17).

Yet, merely wishing to respond in love to God and neighbor is not enough. You find from your past history and all your good resolutions to be a more loving person that you cannot accomplish this consistently unless God comes and sets you free. Jesus himself insisted that you were to remain in his love, united with him in order to bring forth such fruit.

"I am the true vine,
. . . Make your home in me, as I make mine in you.
As a branch cannot bear fruit all by itself,
but must remain part of the vine,
neither can you unless you remain in me . . .
Whoever remains in me, with me in him,
bears fruit in plenty;
for cut off from me you can do nothing" (Jn 15:1-5).

Experiencing the Love of God in Jesus   Seeing your utter inability to be a consistently loving person to all who come into your life, you need a deeper experience given by God's Spirit of your true self in Jesus Christ. This is the person you are in God's eyes. The good news that Jesus preached as the breaking of God's kingdom into your very being is the indwelling love of the Trinity for you in all your particularity. St. Paul discovered that God's infinite, perfect, present and caring love for him was continually being manifested in Christ Jesus, present within him and always dying for him. Experiencing this immense love of Jesus for you, you, too, with St. Paul can live a new life:

> . . . and I live now not with my own life but with the life of Christ who lives in me. The life I now live in this body I live in faith in the Son of God who loved me and who sacrificed himself for my sake (Ga 2:19-20).

Jesus brought the love of the Father to all the broken ones he met by using material aids and techniques so that they were able to come close to him and receive his personalized love for them. In all such techniques Jesus allowed the sick the opportunity to become attentive to God's presence in him. The ease with which Jesus touched all types of sick people and, without complicated methods, healed them, showed the early disciples and those who were open to his total healing presence that Jesus was God's sign of the coming of the kingdom.

Jesus healed, not so much by possessing a psychic energy that passed from him into the sick persons, but rather by being the concrete expression of God's love for his suffering children. Jesus continues to heal you also by his spiritual gaze, his touch, his whole, gentle presence, meeting your crying need. As you yield in faith to God's mysterious presence within Jesus, God's loving, healing presence is released within you.

The secret of Jesus' healing power while he walked this earth lies in the fact that he perfectly imaged the heavenly Father for each sick person whom he met. In the love that he poured out in each look and touch and word, he called the sick to the healing love of God. His Spirit of love allows you to see and experience the presence of the risen Jesus as the

Father's love, living within you, and thus he calls you into the healing of abundant life.

Contemplation Is to Experience God's Love   God extends his healing love to others by pouring his trinitarian love into your heart. It is a powerful but gentle love that permeates and invades your being at all times. True contemplation becomes an ever-increasing consciousness of this exuberant, outpouring love of God as God reveals his energetic love for you in each moment of each event.

As you allow God's love to flow over you like life-giving water, cleansing you of your locked-in self-centeredness, you become transformed into a loving person, open to give love to all whom you meet. You experience daily more and more a strange paradox. As God's love is brought to life within you and you experience a new awareness of your true *you-ness* as being loved so richly and exuberantly by God as Father, Son and Holy Spirit, so you are "impelled" by that inner force of the indwelling Spirit to bring forth by your love for your neighbor God's healing love in the other.

You discover the awesome responsibility to extend Jesus, the healer, into the world around you by the love of God that abounds in your heart (Rm 5:5). As you lovingly care for others, you let the healing power of God pour into their lives. And strangely enough, you, too, as you bring healing to others, experience an increase in new healing love turned toward your own brokenness. Love begets love and healing begets healing and more healing.

Meditation

God is love and Jesus is the image of that love made incarnate. His members are to incarnate his love into their world. Try to reflect on the dignity that is yours, to have been chosen by Jesus to be his follower, to bring forth fruit of love and healing into your world. Pray out quietly chapter

15 of St. John's gospel about the vine and the branches: "You did not choose me, no, I chose you; and I commissioned you to go out and to bear fruit, fruit that will last" (Jn 15:16).

Consider how Jesus chose the twelve apostles and sent them out on their mission of preaching and healing (Lk 9:1-6). He is calling you each day to such a sublime mission of announcing the kingdom of God come upon this earth as you radiate the love of Jesus, the reflected glory of the Father's love for all his children.

> He called the Twelve together and gave them power and authority over all devils and to cure diseases, and he sent them out to proclaim the kingdom of God and to heal. He said to them, "Take nothing for the journey: neither staff, nor haversack, nor bread, nor money; and let none of you take a spare tunic. Whatever house you enter, stay there; and when you leave, let it be from there. As for those who do not welcome you, when you leave their town shake the dust from your feet as a sign to them." So they set out and went from village to village proclaiming the Good News and healing everywhere (Lk 9:1-6).

The Seed of Wheat Falls and Dies

There is a basic law of growth that applies to the human development of body, soul and spirit as well as to all nature around us: "Nothing lives, but something dies. Nothing dies, but something lives." We cannot attain a higher level of human perfection unless we let go of a lower stage. The child must let go of being a child in order to become an adolescent. The young boy or girl must struggle toward adulthood.

Jesus phrased this law of human growth in the lesson about the grain of wheat:

> I tell you, most solemnly,
> unless a wheat grain falls on the ground and dies,
> it remains only a single grain;
> but if it dies,
> it yields a rich harvest.
> Anyone who loves his life loses it;
> anyone who hates his life in this world
> will keep it for the eternal life (Jn 12:24-25).

Jesus taught the necessity of the Son of Man suffering and dying in order to enter glory. He was destined to go to Jerusalem and suffer unto death but he would be raised up on the third day (Mt 16:21-23; Mk 8:31-33; Lk 9:22). But Peter would have none of this talk about suffering. Jesus reproved him with force: "Get behind me, Satan! You are an obstacle in my path, because the way you think is not God's way but man's" (Mt 16:23).

But above all he would live out this law in his own life in order that he might enter into glory and share that glory with us: "And when I am lifted up from the earth, I shall draw all men to myself" (Jn 12:32). Only by "passing over" from his own self-containment and imaging the infinite love of the invisible Father for us, would he be able to share the divine life with us and thus reconcile us back to the Father. Our faith is built upon what happened to him: Death *is* resurrection; love unto death for the other leads us to new life in God and union with the one we love.

I: *The Eucharist*

We have seen so far in our retreat that the purpose of life is to receive God's very own life which is his personalized, trinitarian love for us. As we receive our identity in such love, we are impelled to go forth and share God's life-giving love with other human beings. The heart of all reality is the Trinity. The infinite love within the Trinity, that is, Father loving his Son, in his Spirit and the Son loving in return in the same Spirit of love his Father, that infinite love explodes, as it were. In ecstasy (Greek, *ecstasis,* to stand outside oneself) the uncreated energies of love go forth from the heart of God's essence to be shared in a similar, personalized love of Father, begetting us in his Son in the Spirit, and the Son in us, calling forth the Father through the self-surrendering love poured into our hearts, united to the heart of Jesus Christ through the Spirit.

God begins this pouring himself, his life, into our lives from the Trinity in the incarnation. The trinitarian life comes to us first as God channels all his life through Jesus Christ, the Word of God made flesh, "because God wanted all perfection to be found in him and all things to be reconciled through him and for him" (Col 1:19). St. Paul tells us:

138

"In his body lives the fullness of divinity and in him you too find your own fulfillment" (Col 2:9).

Jesus is the reconciler of all things in the heavens and on the earth. He will restore the world's lost unity as he draws men and women by the loving attraction of his Spirit into his very body. He, at the time of his death and resurrection, in microcosmic fashion, as it were, re-established or reconciled humanity in himself by destroying sin, death and the distorted element in the flesh. The Trinity exalted him in glory (Ph 2:9-11), making him the "eldest of many brothers" (Rm 8:29). At the end of time he will also re-establish all things, raising up the flesh of all mankind by spiritualizing it. He will bring all things completely under his dominion by bestowing the fullness of his divine life upon men for all eternity.

Receiving the Eucharist, Receiving the Trinity   When we receive the Eucharist, the peak of all the sacraments, we touch the glorious, risen Jesus in his new body. Eating his body and drinking his blood, we, in a most marvelous, mysterious way, receive the total Christ, his divinity and humanity. But when Jesus Christ is received, we also receive the Father and his Spirit of love. Who abides in the Son abides in the Father who comes with the Son and his Spirit to dwell within us through the Eucharist (Jn 14:23).

Thus all three mysteries, the Eucharist, the incarnation and the Trinity, are intimately connected and explain each other. The Eucharist brings our oneness with Christ to fullness. And in him our relationship with the Trinity is more than a mere extrinsic adoption into God's family. Jesus shares the very life he enjoys with the Father and the Spirit within the Trinity.

> As I, who am sent by the living Father,
> myself draw life from the Father,
> so whoever eats me will draw life from me.

This is the bread come down from heaven;
not like the bread our ancestors ate:
they are dead,
but anyone who eats this bread will live for ever (Jn 6:57-58).

We are *engrafted* onto his very being as a branch is inserted into the main stem of a vine and becomes one total being (Jn 15:1-6). St. Paul calls it an *incorporation,* a becoming one with the very body of Christ. By his resurrectional life, found in the Eucharist, Jesus shares with us this new life: "When he died, he died, once for all, to sin, so his life now is life with God; and in that way, you too must consider yourselves to be dead to sin but alive for God in Christ Jesus" (Rm 6:10-11).

Receiving the Eucharist has tremendous repercussions on your life. St. Paul tells you that you are united with Christ; therefore you must live *in Christ.* He uses this phrase 164 times to express this intimate, real union with the substance of the total Jesus Christ, true God and true man, risen and glorified, bringing you the power of his Spirit in order that you might die to your selfishness and rise to let him be your Lord and master in every thought, word and deed.

St. Augustine captures the realism of the gospel and the faith of the early Christian communities that gathered to eat of the Bread of Life when he wrote:

Let us rejoice and give thanks that we have become not only Christians but Christ. My brothers, do you understand the grace of God our head? Stand in admiration, rejoice; we have become Christ.

Without losing your identity, but rather now in an exciting, new way you find your uniqueness, your *logos* in the Logos made flesh of God, Jesus Christ, now risen and calling you into your true identity. God made you long ago to be "according to the image and likeness" (Gn 1:26) which in the Eucharist you experience fully to be Jesus Christ. God's plan for you is being realized most fully in your eucharistic union with Jesus Christ within the Trinity:

> They are the ones he chose specially long ago and intended to become true images of his Son, so that his Son might be the eldest of many brothers. He called those he intended for this; those he called he justified, and with those he justified he shared his glory (Rm 8:29-30).

The prayer of Jesus in the Last Supper discourse is being fulfilled in the Eucharist: "Father, may they be one in us, as you are in me and I am in you" (Jn 17:21). The Greek Fathers were quite emphatic when they described this union through the Eucharist with the Trinity. St. Cyril of Alexandria rather forcefully tells us:

> Accordingly we are all one in the Father and in the Son and in the Holy Spirit; one, I say, in unity of relationship of love and concord with God and one another . . . one by conformity in godliness, by communion in the sacred body of Christ, and by fellowship in the one and Holy Spirit and this is a real, physical union.

Union with Each Other   The work of the Holy Spirit in the Eucharist is not only to transform bread and wine into the body and blood of Jesus Christ; he is also effecting a oneness between you and those who are in the body of Christ. As you receive Jesus Christ, the Spirit illumines you to experience more intensely the presence of the love of the Father made manifest through Jesus Christ: "There is one Body, one Spirit, just as you were all called into one and the same hope when you were called. There is one Lord, one faith, one baptism, and one God who is Father of all, over all, through all and within all" (Ep 4:4-6).

The Spirit is the creative, transforming power of God, always uniting what is divided. St. Paul saw the church, whether local or universal, as the *koinonia,* the community of believers, linked together by the Holy Spirit in a unity of faith, sacraments, especially baptism, which reaches its fullness in the Eucharist, and in a loving submission of all to Spirit-guided teaching authority.

As you receive the Lord in the Eucharist, the Spirit gives you a new sense of oneness with those Christians who in that church-body receive the same Lord. You experience that you belong to them and they belong to you and you are all Christ's. But you also are impelled by the love that the Spirit pours into your heart in the Eucharist to go forth from that eucharistic celebration to find your further uniqueness in living for the whole body of Christ that is ultimately to embrace the whole race of saved people of God, the full body of Christ with him as the head.

You open yourself to receive a release of the Spirit's charisms which he wishes you to develop in order that the body of Christ may be built up. The Spirit guides you to love Christ in his Spirit through the love that you have for all human beings. You have now in the Eucharist the power to go outward toward others to form a similar community by being Eucharist, bread broken of all your selfishness in order to give yourself, not only as Jesus did; but now, with Jesus and the Father abiding within you with their Spirit of love, you can do what was impossible for you alone.

You are to receive the total Christ which means to receive every man and woman who comes into your life, for they are meant to be a part of the body of Christ. Whatsoever you do to the least of them you do really to Christ (Mt 25).

> The blessing-cup that we bless is a communion with the blood of Christ, and the bread that we break is a communion with the body of Christ. The fact that there is only one loaf means that though there are many of us, we form a single body because we all have a share in this one loaf (1 Cor 10:16-17).

142

Death to Self   The Eucharist is not only the sacrament of Jesus who gives himself to you and to others who receive him worthily, but it is always his true sacrifice in which he gives himself to the recipients completely and according to their dispositions. This divine bread of life assimilates you into his own life. Through his Spirit he gives the power that you may go forth to become a similar sacrament of self-giving to all whom you meet and are privileged to serve, and a similar sacrifice built upon death to yourself. St. Paul wrote that "a person who eats and drinks without recognizing the Body is eating and drinking his own condemnation" (1 Cor 11:29). This means, not only failure to realize that what you have received is really the body and blood of Christ, but that, by not recognizing your brother and sister outside the eucharistic celebration to be a part of the same body of Christ, you partake of his body in the Eucharist unworthily.

This is an awesome responsibility on the social level to extend the Eucharist into your daily life. Your eucharistic life is to be measured by the fruit of the Spirit that brings forth love in community. You are to "bear with one another charitably, in complete selflessness, gentleness and patience. Do all you can to preserve the unity of the Spirit by the peace that binds you together" (Ep 4:2-3). You have been given very special gifts by the Holy Spirit to build up the body of Christ. You show how much of the total Jesus you have received in the Eucharist by your readiness to go forth from the table of the Lord to be of loving service to others. Such eucharistic love is always patient and kind, never jealous, never boastful or conceited, never rude or selfish. It does not take offense and is not resentful. It takes no pleasure in other people's sins but delights in the truth. It is always ready to excuse, to trust, to hope and to endure whatever comes (1 Cor 13:4-6).

The Cosmic Eucharist   Jesus, by his resurrection, has in-

143

serted himself into the material world in a way in which he could not have been present in his earthly life. He is in the entire, material cosmos as a leaven that is raising the created order into a fullness that redounds to the glory of the Father. But he directs this world to its fulfillment through his living members. Those who worthily have received his body and blood and have received the outpoured Holy Spirit in the Eucharist are to go out and celebrate the eucharistic liturgy of the one high priest, Jesus Christ.

This world around you is not evil. God created it and saw that it was very good (Gn 1:18). Every atom has an important part in the whole of creation. Everything has been meant by the Father to be realized in its uniqueness by becoming a part of the total body of Christ. But it is given to rational human beings to be "co-creators" and "reconcilers" (2 Cor 5:18-19) of the whole world to the Father in cooperation with Jesus Christ risen. Your oneness with Christ, the high priest, was given you in your first baptism. It increases as you allow Jesus to release his Spirit, especially in the climax of all the sacraments, in the Eucharist.

Creation is not yet finished. The cosmic liturgy has not yet reached its complete *com-union* between men and women, united with one another as brothers and sisters of Jesus Christ and children of the one heavenly Father. Human beings are not yet living in the fullness of peace and harmony with the material world, which would bring it to fulfillment according to God's eternal plan. You, however, have entered into that "new creation" with Christ through living the Eucharist (2 Cor 5:17-19). He is asking you to be his ambassador, to join your God-given gifts to his inside presence in whom all things exist and have their being.

Instead of running away from involvement in the activities of the world, you should move "inside" to the Trinity at the heart of matter. With God there is no secular and no sacred world. There is only his uncreated energies of love permeating and invading all of the material world. What you do to make this in any way a better world moves a small part of it forward in the great cosmic liturgy. When the love you experience in the Eucharist becomes the dominant force in your life, then every thought, word and deed is bathed in the light of the indwelling Trinity inside the whole world.

Thus you aid in building up the body of Christ, the church. It is not a gathering of an elite group out of the human race, while the rest of creation is destined for destruction. It is a process of transformation from one level of lower existence unto a higher with greater complexity moving unto greater unity without destroying but rather highlighting the uniqueness of each creature. The only obstacles that hold back the process are the same as those that do not allow us to receive truly the body of Christ fully in the Eucharist: the evils of selfishness, fear and pride.

Meditation

Place yourself reverently in the Upper Room in the presence of Jesus and his disciples at the moment when Jesus gives himself for the first time in human history under the form of bread and wine. See the change that comes over the weak and worldly minded apostles as the Spirit binds them into a new oneness with Jesus and with one another. Read slowly with deep prayer the Last Supper discourse from John 13:1 to 17:26. Seek to discover the Trinity in this eucharistic prayer and make it your life.

II: *Agony in the Garden*

Jesus in the Eucharist at the Last Supper gives himself to his disciples as food and drink. Now, as we contemplate him undergoing his passion and death, we see him "passing

145

over" from self-containment to complete gift of himself to the last drop of blood for love of us and the entire human race.

We have meditated often on the passion and death of Jesus. For one who truly loves Christ, his sufferings and ignominious death are a subject of frequent prayer and reflection. Here we "see" the depths of his love for us as he proves by deeds of suffering unto death the extent of his love. In his passion on the cross we can clearly see the imaged love of the Father incarnated in the humanity of Jesus for love of us.

"To have seen me is to have seen the Father" (Jn 14:9). Now we can enter into the heart of the Father through the suffering heart of the Son "who is nearest to the Father's heart who has made him known" (Jn 1:18). Entering into the darkness of Jesus in his agony in the garden and on the cross, we can know that the Father abides also in suffering darkness as he patiently awaits our loving response to infinite love offered.

Nowhere else in scripture do we see as well what sin is as when we contemplate Jesus made sin for our sake.

> We had all gone astray like sheep,
> each taking his own way,
> and Yahweh burdened him
> with the sins of all of us (Is 53:6).

We can be broken of our self-complacency as we see what our coldness and ingratitude have cost Christ in terms of physical sufferings, but, above all, in personal rejection. God becomes man, emptying himself of his divinity in order to pursue us with God's love, and yet we are untouched by so great a love!

It is in contemplating the sufferings of Jesus that we experience our dignity in his great suffering love. We find the strength in that love to do all that is necessary in order to live a Christian, virtuous life built on love for others. With St. Paul, we can shout out:

So I shall be very happy to make my weaknesses my special boast so that the power of Christ may stay over me, and that is why I am quite content with my weaknesses, and with insults, hardships, persecutions, and the agonies I go through for Christ's sake. For it is when I am weak that I am strong (2 Cor 12:9-10).

We can pray to have a share with Christ crucified in the light of the intoxicating love of Jesus that "tilts" us toward the folly of the cross. And even though sufferings remain still sufferings, we are purified as we suffer to return love for love. Although we suspect the sincerity of our prayer and realize our cowardliness, still we kneel beside our suffering king and master and beg for a share in his sufferings.

Contemplating the Mysteries   Even though we believe that the events of Jesus' suffering and death as narrated in the gospels actually happened in historical time, still we believe that, in the *kairos* time of the everlasting *now* of God's love manifested for us in the human love of Jesus, he is still suffering and dying for us. St. Ignatius in his *Spiritual Exercises* would have us ask ourselves the following questions as we stand intimately inside the passion events:

1. Who is the person who is suffering?
2. What do he and others around him say?
3. What does Christ do?
4. What does he suffer in his humanity and what would he still wish to suffer for you?
5. How does his divinity seemingly hide itself, revealing Jesus to be more human and a greater example for you?
6. How does he suffer these things for you and what ought you to do in return to him by way of suffering?

Gethsemane   Place yourself reverently in the Garden of

Gethsemane. Jesus has just left his three disciples, Peter, James and John, biding them to pray and watch with him. A stone's throw away, in the olive grove, Jesus prostrates himself on the ground. See him there, trembling, sobbing and full of fright. Fear of extreme pain, physical and spiritual, as well as of imminent death comes over him as a new experience.

He, who was so masterful and courageous, now is overcome with heaviness and fright. Gone are the calm majesty, the look of dignity and inner strength. Is this Jesus, the prophet of Nazareth, the great miracle worker, the man who spoke as man never has spoken before, lying in trembling fear?

Agonia in Greek means struggle. Here contemplate Jesus as he struggles to bring his will to accept the sufferings and death that the Father had planned for him on your behalf to gain your love. "For God's foolishness is wiser than human wisdom, and God's weakness is stronger than human strength" (1 Cor 1:25).

St. Thomas Aquinas gives as the first source of Jesus' agony in the garden the vision he had of his approaching sufferings and death. He experiences somehow the lash of the scourge, the crowning with thorns, the humiliations, the thirst, the loss of blood and the extreme sense of abandonment by his heavenly Father: "Yahweh has been pleased to crush him with suffering" (Is 53:10).

Not My Will, But Thine   Jesus struggles to obey the Father on our behalf. So great is his struggle that St. Luke, the physician, observes: "In his anguish he prayed even more earnestly and his sweat fell to the ground like great drops of blood" (Lk 22:44). What love is generated in his heart for you as Jesus prays! "Father, if you are willing, take this cup away from me. Nevertheless, let your will be done, not mine" (Lk 22:42).

148

He really wants to escape dying, and for this he prayed. Yet his love for his Father, his desire to return the infinite love which all his earthly life Jesus had so abundantly experienced, gives him the strength to surrender in love to do his will.

We read that Jesus, so afraid and feeling alone, stumbled to his three disciples as he sought some comfort and support. Yet he found them sleeping: "Why are you asleep? Get up and pray not to be put to the test" (Lk 22:46). Be that angel who appeared to him from heaven to comfort him and to give him strength (Lk 22:44).

The Sins of the World   Another source of suffering came from the experience of Jesus as he undertook the burden of the sins of the world. He who was spotless, without sin, consents to allow all the sins of the world to come upon him.

> And yet ours were the sufferings he bore,
> ours the sorrows he carried.
> But we, we thought of him as someone punished,
> struck by God, and brought low.
> Yet he was pierced through for our faults,
> crushed for our sins.
> On him lies a punishment that brings us peace,
> and through his wounds we are healed (Is 53:4-5).

No one owns your dark and sinful desert. It is all yours and in a way you made it. But Jesus enters into your dark and sinful world and that of every human being. He associates in love with the sins of the world. The innocent Lamb of God who understood the awfulness of sin now has heaped all the filth of the immoral world upon himself. Immersed in a pool of mud and slime, he slashes about to stay on top and yet a force pulls him powerfully into its darkness.

"My soul is sorrowful to the point of death" (Mt 26:38). With his whole being he desires to run away from what the Father is asking of him. And yet he struggles to rise to new

149

heights of human love as he surrenders to be the victim of our sins.

Indifference to Love   As Jesus experienced what terrifying sufferings the Father was asking him to bear on our behalf, a source of new pain and suffering came from his suspicion and perhaps foreknowledge that much of his sufferings would not touch the hearts of many human beings, even those who call themselves his Christian followers.

The greatest pain that a human person can suffer is to love another completely, even unto death, and to experience the rejection of that love or a coldness and indifference to the one offering such love. You can understand the agony which Jesus suffered in knowing that he pursued us with a perfect love only to be spurned by so many.

Is such suffering really worthwhile? Could not the Father have proved the case of his love for mankind without such a total self-giving? Should Jesus hold back in his love, feeling such rejection? Even if he agreed to drink of the cup of suffering, could he not compromise, at least interiorly, to soothe over his great hurts of rejection and indifference?

In his terrible passion, his whole life came before him. So much teaching, so many tiring travels, so much suffering, so many healings and miracles, and yet so few followers even in his own lifetime would understand how great his love for them really was. His own disciples, so slow to learn, would reject him. A sense of loneliness and abandonment, of complete failure and frustration, comes over him. Even the Father's loving face disappears, leaving him mysteriously alone in his temptation to despondency and meaninglessness.

Betrayal by Judas   See the cohort of soldiers and servants of the high priest entering the garden, led by Judas. Jesus had, several years before, told Judas to follow him and he did. Jesus loved him and washed his feet. And now Judas embraces Christ and plants a searing kiss of betrayal on his lips. "Greetings, Rabbi," Judas said and kissed him (Mt 26:50).

Here contemplate your king. His plan of salvation is one of detachment from the riches and power of this world. He chooses freely to be vulnerable and to suffer rejection and humiliations, all because he is meek and humble of heart (Mt 11:29).

Meditation

Place yourself either before the agonizing Jesus in the garden (Mt 26:36-56) or before the prisoner Jesus in the dungeon of Caiphas (Mt 26:57-68), and beg your Master that you may have a share in drinking the cup of sufferings. Pray that you may be found worthy to stand at his side, bearing poverty, humiliations, rejection in order to have more of a part with him, your Lord and master and king!

III: A Crucified God

Nobody cared for a certain group of people, exiled off by themselves on an island. They were lonely, desolate, with no one from the outside to share their misery, no one to help them better their lot. Finally one day a man came, saying that, for love of God, he was going to dedicate his whole life to them. This priest of God worked valiantly for them and one day he addressed them during the Mass as "fellow lepers." Father Damien, when he finally had leprosy, was one with the lepers of Molokai, and this brought him a new confidence and a closer relationship with them. Jesus' suffering makes him one with us. He shares in all our miseries and sufferings. He breaks down any barriers, and we feel capable of approaching him closely with confidence. He draws us with a human heart that has proved its love for us in suffering for us.

> "And when I am lifted up from the earth,
> I shall draw all men to myself" (Jn 12:32).

In the garden of agony Jesus accepted the cup of suffering and drank it to the dregs. Now contemplate your God-man, Jesus Christ, accepting insults and beatings, scourging and a mock crowning with thorns, fatigue, thirst and loss of blood in carrying his cross through the narrow, winding streets of Jerusalem.

His long-awaited hour was nearly upon him: "I have come to bring fire to the earth, and how I wish it were blazing already! There is a baptism I must still receive, and how great is my distress till it is over!" (Lk 12:49-50).

After having been stripped naked and brutally thrown down, Jesus is nailed to the cross. Heavy spikes are driven into his hands and feet and with a dull thud the cross is dropped into the hole prepared for it. His body lurches forward and its weight nearly pulls the body free of the nails, but then it settles back to a three-hour agony of excruciating pain.

King of the Jews   Gaze affectionately at your Lord and master, Jesus Christ, as he slowly enters into the last hours of his earthly life. Forget that it was an event that took place so many centuries ago and see it as taking place now as you stand beside Mary, the mother of Jesus, Mary Magdalene and the beloved disciple, John. This is the king and leader you promised to follow in baptism. Isaiah powerfully describes the Suffering Servant of Yahweh:

> Without beauty, without majesty (we saw him),
> no looks to attract our eyes;
> a thing despised and rejected by men,
> a man of sorrows and familiar with suffering,

a man to make people screen their faces;
he was despised and we took no account of him.
And yet ours were the sufferings he bore,
ours the sorrows he carried.
But we, we thought of him as someone punished,
struck by God, and brought low.
Yet he was pierced through for our faults,
crushed for our sins.
On him lies a punishment that brings us peace,
and through his wounds we are healed (Is 53:2-5).

But it is in the hymn of the messianic Psalm 22 that the
Spirit of God brings us to a new understanding of Jesus' love
for us. The Spirit reveals to us the infinite depths of the
Father's love for us as we contemplate the Suffering Servant,
Jesus. The first part is the cry of Jesus to his Father in the
darkness of abandonment that came over his human consciousness. The sky darkened and the raucous soldiers
stopped their ribaldry and mocking jests. Earth, sky and air
suddenly froze in a mute stare at the white figure hanging on
the cross. A cry pierced the darkened silence:

My God, my God, why have you deserted me?
How far from saving me, the words I groan!
I call all day, my God, but you never answer,
all night long I call and cannot rest (Ps 22:1-2).

"Eli . . . Eli . . . " At that moment the Father of Jesus
who had always been a light, bathing him with his smiling
love, now seemed clouded in fierce darkness. How Jesus
must have thrilled at his baptism and at the transfiguration
to have heard words of loving approval from his Father:
"This is my Son, the Beloved; my favor rests on him" (Mt
3:17). But now it is as though the Father's wrath is poured
out against him; Jesus feels the quagmire of the world's sinful filth suck him down and cover him with darkness.

Jeremiah had predicted the anger of God and Jesus
becomes the image of that storm:

> Now a storm of Yahweh breaks,
> a tempest whirls,
> it bursts over the head of the wicked;
> the anger of Yahweh will not turn aside
> until he has performed and carried out,
> the decision of his heart.
> You will understand this in the days to come (Jr 30:23-24).

As Jesus surrenders completely to his Father's will, soft rays of light move toward the darkness just as the first sign of dawn with its velvet touch dissolves the darkness. In Jesus' despairing abandonment, groping to look again upon the countenance of the Father he adored so profoundly, he experiences the paradox he had preached to others: "Happy those who mourn: they shall be comforted" (Mt 5:5).

> Do not stand aside, Yahweh,
> O my strength, come quickly to my help. . . .
> Then I shall proclaim your name to my brothers,
> praise you in full assembly;
> you who fear Yahweh, praise him!
> Entire race of Jacob, glorify him!
> Entire race of Israel, revere him!
> For he has not despised
> or disdained the poor man in his poverty,
> has not hidden his face from him
> but has answered him when he called (Ps 22:19,22-24).

Love Is Brokenness   He who was constantly bathed in the warm light of the Father's love now gropes alone in terrifying darkness. Not even a slight ray of hope to dispel his aloneness! Fear, doubt and rejection come over him in his last hour. Deeper down into his heart he pushes to surrender in emptying love to his absent Father: "Do not stand aside, Yahweh. O my strength, come quickly to my help" (Ps 22:19).

In such complete brokenness of body, soul and spirit, Jesus surrenders himself to the Father in complete self-giving to return the Father's total gift of himself. As the soft morning dawn gently lifts the darkness from the face of the earth to let the sun burst into being with full radiance, so the light of the Father's love softly falls upon Jesus' broken spirit to drive away the darkness of despair and abandonment.

Jesus again sees the bright light of the Father's countenance. "It is accomplished," whispers the Father. "Yes, Father, it is accomplished. Father, into your hands I commend my spirit." The Father is completely pleased by the Son because he has become the fully expressed word of the eternal mind, perfectly expressing the Father's love in human language of suffering unto death: "As the Father has loved me, so I have loved you" (Jn 15:9).

Your Response   This is the wisdom of God, chosen to confound the logic of men. It is the folly of the cross that can never be understood except by the logic of love that is tilted toward the cross of suffering and self-sacrifice. Stand at the foot of the cross and watch the soldier pierce Jesus' side with a spear: ". . . and immediately there came out blood and water" (Jn 19:34).

Not only does the pierced heart of Jesus prove to you his sacrificial love, but now Jesus, passing over into death, is glorified and can pour out his Spirit (Jn 7:39) upon all mankind. The Spirit is life-giving water that purifies your heart in its deepest layers of consciousness as he reveals to you in contemplation the love of Jesus for you.

Enter into that pierced heart and be regenerated by the outpoured Spirit. Let that Spirit, as the prophet Ezekiel foretold, give you "a new heart, and put a new spirit in you" (Ez 36:26). Let that Spirit remove your heart of stone and replace it with a new heart of flesh.

> If we have died with him, then we shall live with him.
> If we hold firm, then we shall reign with him.
> If we disown him, then he will disown us.

ALONE WITH THE ALONE

We may be unfaithful, but he is always faithful,
for he cannot disown his own self (2 Tm 2:11-13).

Meditation

1. Prayerfully reflect on Isaiah 53:1-12 and on Psalm 22. Pause wherever you feel most centered upon Jesus crucified. Strive to contemplate rather than meditate on words or ideas. Let the Spirit move you to understand in a new depth the burning, trinitarian love for you as you experience the gentle, emptying love of Father, Son and Holy Spirit in Jesus poured out on the cross.

2. Reflect on the last seven "words" that Jesus uttered on the cross:

> a) "Father, forgive them; they do not know what they are doing" (Lk 23:34).
>
> b) "Today you will be with me in paradise" (Lk 23:43).
>
> c) "Woman, this is your son . . ." (Jn 19:26).
>
> d) "My God, my God, why have you deserted me?" (Mk 15:34).
>
> e) "I am thirsty" (Jn 19:28).
>
> f) "It is accomplished" (Jn 19:30).
>
> g) "Father, into your hands I commit my spirit" (Lk 23:46).

SEVENTH DAY

The Life of Glory

Have you ever wondered why it is that in a retreat, as well as in the liturgical year, we find it difficult to move with ease from the passion and death of Jesus into contemplating the mysteries of the risen Lord? One must admit that it is easier to imagine Christ physically undergoing great sufferings and pain and finally death from crucifixion than to picture Jesus in his newly risen presence. If we dwell too much on the physical aspects of the resurrectional apparitions, we miss the mystery and cling, not to the totally risen Jesus, but to a "resuscitated" Christ.

In a way Jesus is the same person in the resurrection as he was before his death. Yet in a very real sense he is totally different: "I was dead and now I am to live for ever and ever . . ." (Rv 1:18). We are in need of receiving from God's Spirit a new knowledge that is experiential. St. Paul made this his constant prayer: "All I want is to know Christ and the power of his resurrection and to share his sufferings by reproducing the pattern of his death. That is the way I can hope to take my place in the resurrection of the dead" (Ph 3:10-11).

This is a growth process that has no end. It summarizes the paradoxical purpose of our life: *Death is resurrection;* love is suffering but it also is joy. Lose your life and you will find it. Love brings uniqueness and distinction, yet it unites through union.

Antinomy   Perhaps we can break the stalemate in our pondering the mysteries of the resurrection and gain new insight by reflecting on the following Japanese *koan*. A koan is an antinomy, a paradoxical statement that has little meaning when one ponders it using only rational powers. Insight cuts through the logical paradox to reveal a truth that is no longer *either/or* but now admits of *both/and.*

Once Nansen, who was the spiritual leader of a large Buddhist monastery of monks, discovered the monks from the Eastern and the Western halls arguing about a cat in their midst. "Can any one of you give me a word?" asked Nansen. No one replied, so Nansen quickly took his sword and killed the cat. When his disciple, Joshu, returned in the evening, Nansen told him what he had done. Joshu immediately took off his straw sandals, put them on top of his head and left the room. The master said, "If you had been here, I could have spared the cat."

What is the meaning of this strange story? Sin has built walls between all men and women. We live in a dualism of subject versus object. The Father killed his Son on a cross to cut through that dualism and thus to lead us back to the true unity among us in which cats and human beings are all united in the Son of God. The killing sword of Nansen was meant to be life-giving. The death of Jesus conquers death and sin, separation and division, and restores us to that original unity and harmony of all creatures through love.

Joshu's action transcends the dualistic relativism that believes the head is more noble than the feet and sandals are things dirty and not attractive and, therefore, should have no relationship with a person's face and head.

The Cross Is Resurrection   As we experience a sharing in the death and resurrection of Jesus we come to know that death through love is directly linked to glory. Dualistic thinking holds that we suffer unpleasant things and die.

Then we eventually, in a time-space projection, enter into heaven, glory and resurrection. Pray for knowledge to experience that God is in the suffering as well as in the glory. Death by love does not lead to your resurrection, but death is resurrection! Jesus is the link that makes this possible. He brings the two together in your life as you experience his death-resurrection.

I: *Jesus Risen*

Jesus, dying on the cross for love of you and all human beings, *passes over* into his new, resurrectional existence, not after three days, but immediately as he dies. Death is resurrection! Love, when it reaches its peak, moves immediately from death to aloneness to enter into a new union with the one loved.

St. Paul writes: "Jesus . . . was put to death for our sins and raised to life to justify us" (Rm 4:25). Jesus "died and was raised to life" (2 Cor 5:15) for us that we might have eternal life. He now can share with us his divine life by releasing his Spirit of love so that we can know by a new knowledge how infinite God's love for us is as imaged in Jesus' death on the cross.

A New Time   Jesus risen lives in a new time. It is the *kairos* or salvific time in which we can enter into his victory over sin and death and be healed of our death-dealing isolation and self-centeredness. We can meet Jesus risen only by entering into his new existence. That is why we cannot study his resurrectional apparitions merely as historical happenings alone. Men and women in the New Testament witness to their encounter with the risen Jesus by faith. Jesus risen was able to send them the vivifying Spirit who could lead them into the *now* experience of Jesus raising them beyond sin and death into a share of his resurrection and eternal life.

Jesus meets us also in his eternal *now kairos* moment which touches us in our historical *(chronos)* moment. Into this moment of brokenness in our history Jesus comes with the Father to lift us to a similar "resurrection" unto new life as in his Spirit we live out of love.

The apostles did not yearn in nostalgia for the historical past times in which they had experienced Jesus. They were experiencing him in a progression forward to a new way in which they could live in his victory always, night and day. If they only wished, they need never be separated from the indwelling Father, Son and Holy Spirit. No longer was Jesus physically present to them as before in one limited place in Palestine. Now wherever they went, they carried this transforming, conquering power within them.

A New Presence   Although Jesus accommodated himself to his followers by assuming a form in which they could still recognize him, he also pushed them to "see" him by faith. To meet Jesus as the new creation, the disciples needed to make the step gradually from the historical Jesus to the risen Jesus. Thus those eyewitnesses had a direct and personal experience of a "bodied" Jesus. It was because they did, that successive generations of Christian believers, including ourselves in the 20th century, could be brought into a "faithful" experience of Jesus existing in glory.

When Mary Magdalene met the risen Jesus in a physical form that she thought was that of the gardener, she recognized Jesus in his word, "Mary," spoken to her. To the early Christian community, though, he was saying (through a paraphrase of John 20:17): "Do not cling to me as you formerly knew and loved me. . . . Go and find the brothers and there you will also discover me in the only way I wish to be present to you."

Again the message of the church in the appearance of Jesus to the apostle Thomas is:

"You believe because you can see me.

Happy are those who have not seen and yet believe" (Jn 20:29).

St. Luke explores this truth of Jesus present to the Christian community in a new way in the story of Jesus and the two disciples at Emmaus. The Evangelist wishes to teach the necessity of Christ's sufferings as a necessary part of his glorification. He argues this by having Jesus as the Word in scripture explain himself in terms of the messianic predictions in the Old Testament that clearly presented the Messiah's glory as part of his suffering servant role. Christ's glory was the goal and purpose of his sufferings:

"You foolish men! So slow to believe the full message of the prophets! Was it not ordained that the Christ should suffer and so enter into his glory?" Then, starting with Moses and going through all the prophets, he explained to them the passages throughout the scriptures that were about himself (Lk 24:25-27).

But if we examine the details presented by Luke, we see a deeper teaching. Although Jesus is physically present to them, nevertheless, their eyes were kept from recognizing him because they were still judging, not by faith within the context of the Word's presence and action to the community of God's people, but by the physical side of the Word.

It was in the "breaking of the bread" that their eyes were opened to recognize Jesus present to them. Luke and the early church are saying that there is a new presence of the risen Jesus that goes beyond his physical presence. The Word of God is present and recognized as such, not by seeing him, but by hearing the Christian community that gathers together through Jesus' Spirit and that speaks the word in continuity with God's revelation in tradition, both of

161

the Old and New Covenants. There can be no contact with the glorious, risen Jesus except in his body, the church that in space and time now makes him present to us.

Not only is Jesus present in glory in the community's preaching of the word but he is also freshly present in the church's *doing*. St. Paul gives an early belief in the church's eucharistic *re-presentation* of Jesus for the believers:

> Until the Lord comes, therefore, every time you eat this bread and drink this cup, you are proclaiming his death, and so anyone who eats the bread or drinks the cup of the Lord unworthily will be behaving unworthily towards the body and blood of the Lord. Everyone is to recollect himself before eating this bread and drinking this cup; because a person who eats and drinks without recognizing the Body is eating and drinking his own condemnation (1 Cor 11:26-29).

The Victory of Jesus   The good news that pervades every page of the New Testament is that Jesus has died for love of us but is now risen and lives in us so that we, too, need never live under bondage of sin and death to God's life. We are capable of entering into his glorious, eternal life by confessing our sins and living only for him as our Lord. He is the first fruits of the new creation. He is the new Adam who brings us a rebirth to new life through his Holy Spirit.

> It was for no reason except his own compassion that he saved us, by means of the cleansing water of rebirth and by renewing us with the Holy Spirit which he has so generously poured over us through Jesus Christ our saviour . . . to become heirs looking forward to inheriting eternal life (Tt 3:5-7).

Jesus shares his victory with you as you encounter his resurrectional presence within you at all times, always dying for you that you might die to self and rise to him.

Jesus Is Lord   St. Paul gives the title of *Lord (Kyrios)* to the risen Jesus to designate that after his resurrection Jesus is totally one with Yahweh. He is in glory and he exercises a royal sovereignty and dominion over the entire cosmos. He is the *Pantocrator,* the almighty Lord of the universe, by being inserted into matter in his spiritualized presence, and he is reconciling the world to the Father by bringing it to its full completion.

> He is the image of the unseen God
> and the first-born of all creation,
> for in him were created
> all things in heaven and on earth:
> everything visible and everything invisible,
> Thrones, Dominations, Sovereignties, Powers —
> all things were created through him and for him.
> Before anything was created, he existed,
> and he holds all things in unity.
> Now the Church is his body,
> he is its head.
> As he is the beginning,
> he was first to be born from the dead,
> so that he should be first in every way;
> because God wanted all perfection
> to be found in him
> and all things to be reconciled through him and for him,
> everything in heaven and everything on earth,
> when he made peace
> by his death on the cross (Col 1:15-20).

Although he is in glory, interceding for us at the right hand of the Father, you must break through the dualistic relativism and avoid thinking of him "up there." The power of the Holy Spirit raises Jesus to a new transcendence, one with the Father in majesty, power and glory. This power of transcendence is also a power of immanence that places Jesus risen "inside" our material world. Not only is he everywhere as the total Jesus Christ, but he is directing the cosmos of all creatures toward the omega point that is ultimately himself in his completed body, the church.

163

Ambassadors of Christ   Jesus brings all things into completion by sending us his Holy Spirit who imparts to us the very "uncreated energies" of God, divinizing us into his children. As Jesus risen meets us in the human context of our daily lives and we surrender to live in love toward him and our neighbor, we, too, even now pass from death to life. We share in his resurrectional life. Our final resurrection is already being realized in a limited way as we are swept up into his transforming power of love.

To the degree that we have entered into his death-resurrection, we will be able to extend the resurrectional, transforming power of Jesus into the material world around us. Jesus risen becomes more risen in his body, the church, as we and others allow him to effect the reconciliation of the divided world through our creative efforts. He hands on to us this great work of reconciliation of a world that is torn by dissension and separation.

> And for anyone who is in Christ, there is a new creation; the old creation has gone, and now the new one is here. It is all God's work of handing on this reconciliation. In other words, God in Christ was reconciling the world to himself, not holding men's faults against them, and he has entrusted to us the news that they are reconciled. So we are ambassadors for Christ; it is as though God were appealing through us, and the appeal that we make in Christ's name is: to be reconciled to God (2 Cor 5:17-20).

Your work is most important in the eyes of God. It is through your cooperation with the energies of God that this world can evolve into its full transformation into Christ's body, the church. Whatever work you do to make this world a bit better, on any level of political, social, scientific, technological, artistic endeavor, you are contributing to the fulfillment of this world.

And to the degree that you die to self and live unto

Christ by loving service to all whom you meet, to that degree you have become risen with Jesus. Death is resurrection, and Jesus is the way that makes it possible through the mystery of living in the love of his Spirit.

Meditation

Place yourself before Jesus in the three resurrectional appearances:

1. Jn 20:11-18. Mary Magdalene hears Jesus call her name, "Mary!" and then she knows that the person she thought was the gardener is really her risen master. "Do not cling to me . . . but go and find the brothers and tell them: I am ascending to my Father . . ."

2. Lk 24:13-35. The two disciples meet Jesus on the road to Emmaus but do not recognize him. He enlightens their spiritual eyes by explaining scripture. He had to die in order to enter into glory. Death is resurrection! But they fully recognize him in the breaking of the bread, in the church's supreme act of giving Jesus in death-resurrectional love that we are to give to each other in the community of the church.

3. Jn 20:24-29. Jesus poured out his Spirit on some of the believing apostles on the eve of the resurrection. Doubting Thomas failed to receive the Spirit and lived still on a dualistic level of subject-object. Jesus meets his demands and Thomas learns to believe by faith that Jesus is his Lord and God. "You believe because you can see me. Happy are those who have not seen and yet believe."

II: *The Indwelling Spirit*

The Holy Spirit, like Jesus risen, cannot be objectivized. The Spirit can only be the Gift of the Father sent to us by the risen Lord. Such a gift of love can only be in the realm of an experienced power of love that transforms us into people who love by that inner power.

The work of the resurrected Christ can never be separated from the Holy Spirit. The Spirit is a special power, distinct from the power of the risen Jesus. Yet he is tied to Jesus: "We know that he lives in us by the Spirit that he has given us" (1 Jn 3:24). The Spirit in the New Testament is presented to us as the new way of existence and action by the risen Jesus. They cannot be separated. The Spirit's work is to be Christ's life-giving Spirit to the world. He draws us into Christ, into his body. He divinizes us, making us true children of God (Rm 8:15; Ga 4:6) and new creatures in Christ Jesus (2 Cor 5:17).

The Work of the Holy Spirit   Before his death, Jesus had promised to send the Spirit of truth to his disciples to be with them forever (Jn 14:15-17). This coming of the Spirit should be a cause of joy because Jesus' coming to them in a new way through the Spirit was dependent upon his leaving them in earthly form (Jn 16:7).

The Spirit would give testimony on Jesus' behalf and would teach all disciples all that Jesus had said and done (Jn 14:26). But primarily the Spirit would dwell within us, making our bodies temples of God (1 Cor 3:16; 1 Cor 6:19). He brings us into direct contact with the spiritualized body-person of Jesus risen and convinces us that both Jesus and the Father also abide within us (Jn 14:21-23).

God's Spirit and our spirit bear united witness that we truly are children of God (Rm 8:15). By the Spirit of the risen Jesus we live now according to the inner principle of life that is Jesus risen, inseparable from his Spirit. As we yield to the Spirit's direction from within, the Spirit sanctifies us by a continued regeneration (Jn 3:3-5). He does this by being the loving force, always uniting us with the Father and the Son, and yet he differentiates us as unique persons made other than the Father and the Son.

Praying in the Spirit   As Jesus is risen and permeates all things, so the Holy Spirit is constantly one with him as the Spirit opens us up to his loving, resurrectional presence. Prayer, as the atmosphere in which we experience the ever-now love of Jesus risen but always dying for us, becomes more an operation of the Spirit within us and less anything we do by way of "saying prayers" or talking to God.

St. Paul tells us that the Spirit prays powerfully within us:

> The Spirit too comes to help us in our weakness. For when we cannot choose words in order to pray properly, the Spirit himself expresses our plea in a way that could never be put into words, and God who knows everything in our hearts knows perfectly well what he means, and that the pleas of the saints expressed by the Spirit are according to the mind of God (Rm 8:26-27).

The Spirit of love pushes us to enter more and more deeply into our hearts. He leads us beyond the idols concerning God that we have built up over years of prayer. Down come the masks and posturing as we are filled with an abiding sense of sin and sorrow, even fear, of the past, and distrust of our sincerity in the future. Broken of our pride and independent egoism, we cry out with urgency in our poverty for healing.

More positively the Spirit teaches us to pray in spirit and truth by allowing us, through his increased infusion of faith, hope and love, to experience that we are being divinized by grace and truly belong to God's family (2 P 1:4).

Part of experiencing a share in God's life is an inner knowledge of holy scripture that springs forth as a two-edged sword, cleaving our own way of thinking from the Spirit of

God's understanding (Heb 4:12). We begin to know the inner mysteries of the Father's love for us as revealed by the teachings and actions of Jesus (Jn 14:26).

Jesus begins to live in our hearts through faith, being built on love, so we "will with all the saints have strength to grasp the breadth and the length, the height and the depth" of the knowledge of Jesus (Ep 3:18).

Praying in the Spirit ultimately becomes a life in which every thought, word and deed is lived completely for the glory of the heavenly Father. As in the life of Jesus, so our life becomes one of abandonment at each moment and in each event. Prayer is, in a word, surrendering love of ourselves to God who has totally given himself to us in his Son, Jesus. The Spirit convinces us "that by turning everything to their good, God co-operates with all those who love him" (Rm 8:28).

Fruit of the Spirit "Where the Spirit is, there is freedom" (2 Cor 3:17). As we seek in honesty and sincerity to be guided by the indwelling Spirit, we progressively are "born of the Spirit" (Jn 3:6). Yielding to the experience of being loved infinitely by God's family of Father, Son and Holy Spirit, we begin to enjoy new freedom as children of God. We lose our haunting fears and anxieties as the Spirit releases new power in us to love God at all times and to show that love in humble service to our neighbor.

The Spirit brings forth the infallible fruit that we are growing in him as we see such fruit manifested in our daily relationships. More intense is the love we show to others, especially toward those who before would have been considered by us as "unlovable." We are at peace and filled with joy. Patience and gentleness are a constant trait amid trials:

> What the Spirit brings is very different: love, joy, peace, patience, kindness, goodness, trustfulness, gentleness and self-control. There can be no law against things like that, of

course. You cannot belong to Christ Jesus unless you crucify all self-indulgent passions and desires. Since the Spirit is our life, let us be directed by the Spirit (Ga 5:22-25).

Building the Church   Jesus risen poured out his Spirit upon his twelve apostles to transform them into a new creation, his body, the church. Filled with the Spirit, they went forth to witness to the inner transformation they had experienced by preaching and witnessing to the risen Jesus and by performing signs and miracles. They spoke in the universal language of love and healed dissensions and disharmony wherever they discovered them separating brother from brother.

They were aware of the power to bind and loose, given them by Jesus, but exercised by them as they were led by the Spirit: "It has been decided by the Holy Spirit and by ourselves" (Ac 15:28).

Not only do the apostles possess charisms to build up the body of Christ, but each Christian receives unique gifts for special functions in the church (Rm 12:4; 1 Cor 12:12-27). Each part of the body is harmoniously knit together through the energy that comes from Jesus Christ in his Spirit.

So we, too, have been called to a particular role within the body of Christ. This necessitates a continued purification and conversion away from dark egoism to be led consistently by the inner light of the Spirit of the risen Jesus. By saying continuously "yes" in love to the leadings of Jesus' Spirit, we will become "reconcilers" to bring all things back to the Father.

We already know the talents which God has given us. Everything we do in love has a power from God's Spirit to add to the building of the total Jesus Christ. In all the details of our lives God's Spirit is operating. As we become more docile and sensitive to his presence and guidance in our every thought, word and deed, we will be used by the Spirit to transform the world into Christ.

Come, Holy Spirit   St. Paul exhorts us: "Be filled with the Spirit" (Ep 5:18). This is what being "baptized" by Jesus Christ in his Spirit means. This is only possible if we truly surrender to the direction of the Holy Spirit. Such a desire must be expressed in our lives not only *affectively* but also *effectively*. Wanting to be led by the Spirit means also a great desire to uproot selfishness and pride from our lives. Wanting to follow St. Paul's advice, "What God wants is for you all to be holy" (1 Th 4:3), means a constant vigilance to attack and destroy any sinful desires in our hearts.

As you purify your heart, you will see God the Trinity dwelling within you. True experience of the indwelling Trinity and true baptism in the Holy Spirit will always be measured by the degree that you allow the Spirit to transfigure you into love, which manifests itself by your going out in loving service toward others. True love of God will always be a true love for other human beings. Your growth, both as a human being and as a Christian, can be measured infallibly by your loving service toward all who somehow come into your life. It is through you that Christ's Spirit builds up his body and this happens when the love of the Spirit of the risen Jesus impels you to be love to others.

> Let us love one another
> since love comes from God
> and everyone who loves is begotten by God and knows God.
> Anyone who fails to love can never have known God. . . .
> . . . as long as we love one another
> God will live in us
> and his love will be complete in us. . . .
> God is love
> and anyone who lives in love
>   lives in God,
> and God lives in him (1 Jn 4:7-16).

Meditation

Enter prayerfully into the first Pentecost experience in the Jerusalem community: Acts 2:1-47. You are much like the first followers of Jesus. You like they know that there is an urgent need for something to happen if you are to live up to the promises and commands of Jesus. They awaited the outpouring of the Spirit by eight days of preparation by prayer and fasting: "Ask, and it will be given to you; search, and you will find; knock, and the door will be opened to you . . ." (Lk 11:9-10). Ask the Father in Jesus' name and he will release the Spirit within you.

Offer yourself to be a channel of that Spirit of love to all who enter your life. Have the courage to pray the prayer of that first Christian community: " '. . . help your servants to proclaim your message with all boldness, by stretching out your hand to heal and to work miracles and marvels through the name of your holy servant Jesus.' As they prayed, the house where they were assembled rocked; they were all filled with the Holy Spirit and began to proclaim the word of God boldly" (Ac 4:29-31).

III: *Transforming Light*

Most retreats end shortly after the retreatant has prayerfully meditated on the passion and death of Christ with a quick consideration given to his resurrection. It is important that we carry the spirit of our retreat into our daily life and see that life is a process of growing into the transfiguring light of Christ who abides within us with his Father in his Spirit.

We are called to be contemplatives, who easily and everywhere "see" the *Shekinah,* the glory of God, especially as revealed by the gloriously risen Jesus Christ inside our material world. Jesus is to be discovered by us as an inner, transfiguring light, directing us how to live in his light and how to be transfigured from darkness to light.

In his transforming light we not only can see his glory, shining through in all material creation, but we are impelled by the divinizing Spirit of Jesus to go forth and be Christ's light to the world that still lies in darkness. Our work is contemplative as we strive to transfigure the material world into the glorified body of Christ.

The Shekinah of God   In the Old and New Testaments God's loving and communicating presence to humanity is called his *Shekinah* or indwelling glory. He, who is light, in whom there is no darkness (1 Jn 1:5), can never be seen by us human beings: "No one has ever seen God" (1 Jn 4:12). God told Moses: "You cannot see my face for man cannot see me and live" (Ex 33:21).

And yet God loves his material creation and sees that it is very good (Gn 1:31). He creates man according to his own image and likeness (Gn 1:26) so that human beings, alone of all material creatures, possess spiritual faculties to communicate with God. Like the sun that communicates its light and heat by rays, so God shares his very being with us by his uncreated energies of love actively present in all creatures. The good news is that God is not far from us and we can truly share in his communicated divine life, "since it is in him that we live, and move, and exist" (Ac 17:28).

God's sustaining presence is discovered in his Logos through whom all things are created (Jn 1:3; Col 1:16). God's loving energies bathe the whole universe and charge it with his infinite love and grandeur.

But it is only when God's Word (Logos) "pitches his tent and dwells among us" (Jn 1:14) that we are able to see God's glory fully revealed in the person of Jesus Christ.

And we saw his glory,
the glory that is his as the only Son of the Father,
full of grace and truth. . . .

172

Indeed, from his fullness we have, all of us, received —
yes, grace in return for grace (Jn 1:14-16).

Transfigured Jesus   The intensity of God's divine,
trinitarian life always shone as a transfiguring, inner light of
glory in Jesus. Yet at times this light blazed forth and suf-
fused him totally as transfigured light. This happened at his
transfiguration on Mount Tabor (Mk 9:1-7; Mt 17:1-8; Lk
9:28-36).

This same transfigured Christ is implanted within us in
our baptism as an embryonic life. His glorious light is to
blaze forth as we yield to his risen, glorious presence within
us. Jesus cannot be more transfigured and glorious than he
is in our baptism. But it is we, like the apostles, who do not
quite see him in all his transfiguring light at all times: "There
in their presence he was transfigured" (Mk 9:2).

As we die to the darkness of self-centeredness in our
life, the light of Christ is not only seen by us, but we begin to
experience his transfiguring of us into his same glorious
light.

Light from Light   By his Spirit living within us, Jesus lives
in his risen glory within us. Like a leaven, he permeates
from within our every part: body, mind and spirit. Each moment is given to us so that we may surrender ourselves to his
inner light and be transformed also through a sharing even
now of his glorious resurrection.

His light within us is not a physical light. It is an inner,
transcendent light that has no form. Yet it is something that
can be experienced as "localized" in our "heart," in the
deepest levels of our consciousness. He is totally present
within us and we experience him in all his glorified divinity-
humanity.

This is the gift of contemplation which the Spirit of the
risen Jesus pours into our hearts by the infused gifts of faith,

173

hope and love. Faith rips off the outer covering of each creature that hides the face of God in so many diverse forms. It leads us to a knowledge of how God is in all creatures and all creatures are in him. We intuit the divine redemptive plan of how Christ in this or that event is reconciling a segment of the broken world into his body unto the glory of the Father.

Hope allows us, in spite of our remaining darkness and sinfulness, to open up to God's loving presence in a childlike abandonment of our weakness to his almighty strength. With him, we firmly believe in the context of our real, nitty-gritty world that all things are possible with God and can work unto good (Rm 8:28).

Love is receiving God's immense love and in total surrender giving ourselves back to him in loving service to him and all human beings. Love becomes a state of contemplating God as we continually experience in each moment his love, and in our love we desire to work out a returned love that is the gift of ourselves to him.

You Are the Light of the World   As we yield to the transforming power of Jesus' Spirit in a continued death to selfishness, that same Spirit urges us to let the transfiguring light of Jesus pour through our transfigured oneness with him to become his light to the world around us. Jesus teaches us in a contemplative experience that admits of an infinity of growth: "I am the light of the world; anyone who follows me will not be walking in the dark; he will have the light of life" (Jn 8:12). If you believe in him and obey his inner, directing light, you shall not remain any longer in darkness (Jn 12:46).

Our hearts are enlightened and our whole being is made lightsome (Mt 6:22). This inner light of the indwelling Trinity suffuses our entire being as we joyfully experience in every thought, word and deed the exhilarating joy of being a

174

child of God. God has called us "out of darkness into his wonderful light" (1 P 2:9).

But Jesus tells us that, as we share in his transfiguring light, so we are to be a transfiguring light to others.

> You are the light of the world. A city built on a hill-top cannot be hidden. No one lights a lamp to put it under a tub; they put it on the lampstand where it shines for everyone in the house. In the same way your light must shine in the sight of men, so that, seeing your good works, they may give the praise to your Father in heaven (Mt 5:14-16).

Serving a Broken World   As we live in the light of the risen Savior, we humbly receive Christ's call to go forth into a broken, sinful, darkened world to be a transforming light of God's love to all persons we are privileged to meet and lovingly serve. Now everywhere we look, we see the forming of the body of Christ. Like Mary, we stretch ourselves to be used to fashion the body of Christ by the raw material that God puts into our hands.

We see Christ laughing in the joyful. We see his face etched in suffering in those who suffer. The more defaced is the image of Christ in human beings the more we give a loving touch and an embrace of love to drive away darkness and transfigure our brother and sister into the light of Christ.

God has consecrated us to share in the "royal priesthood" of Christ by our baptism and confirmation. We share in the transfiguring power of Jesus' Spirit of love that can breathe over a world of rocks and roses, fish and fowl, streams and oceans, valleys and mountains, the broken and maimed human beings of this world and say: "This is *my* body!" We breathe the name of Jesus over each person we meet and believe that Jesus is now more risen in glory because his light has gone out from us to another, dispelling in some little way the darkness of the world.

Jesus now lives in this world through us. He transforms

the world into his body as we cooperate to bring him alive in the outcast, the poor, the sick and the suffering, the lonely and the imprisoned.

> "For I was hungry and you gave me food; I was thirsty and you gave me drink; I was a stranger and you made me welcome; naked and you clothed me, sick and you visited me, in prison and you came to see me. Then the virtuous will say to him in reply, 'Lord, when did we see you hungry and feed you; or thirsty and give you drink? When did we see you a stranger and make you welcome; naked and clothe you; sick or in prison and go to see you?' And the King will answer, 'I tell you solemnly, in so far as you did this to one of the least of these brothers of mine, you did it to me' " (Mt 25:35-40).

A Cosmic Liturgy   If we are experiencing the light of Christ transfiguring us from within, we will realize that the whole material world is "transfigurable" into Christ. The spiritual presence of Christ no longer competes with our material activities. Rather, we contemplate the light of God everywhere in the very action of bringing that light to full realization by action done in Christlike love.

No longer are there areas in our life or in the world that are "secular" or profane, as if closed out from the permeating, loving presence of the Trinity. Now all things are sacred since we can see "Jesus Christ, shining diaphanously through the whole world," to quote Tielhard de Chardin. We begin to understand the challenging statement of Dietrich Bonhoeffer's words: "In Christ we are offered the possibility of partaking in the reality of God and in the reality of the world, but not in the one without the other."

Resurrectional hope is social and historical. Jesus is *now* transfiguring the world into a sharing in his glorious body, but through our cooperation. He calls us to be "reconcilers" of the broken world (2 Cor 5:18). It is the whole, material world and not merely a small, elite group of "saved people" that is to be the body of Christ. God never creates to destroy but only to transform. From matter to spirit to Christ is God's evolutive plan in Christ.

We should vie with the humanists and all others who seek to make this world a better place for all human beings to develop the rich potential that God has put into each unique person. Whatever we add through our loving service in the field of religion, politics, science, art, recreation or family life must be seen as an opportunity to build the world into the body of Christ.

A Transfigured World   The world is far from complete and fulfilled. There is still much darkness and sinfulness in us. God through Mary entered into a filthy, sordid world that had much ugliness and there his Word took on flesh. It was the real but unfinished world into which Christ came as the light. It is the same existential world that you are to enter and bring the transfiguring light of the risen Jesus.

God calls us inwardly to let the trinitarian energies transform us into sharers of divine light and glory. But it is also outwardly that God sends us into a suffering world to become his transfiguring light wherever we may encounter darkness. The heavenly Jerusalem is now piercing through the suffering shadows of a world still groaning before it has been transfigured into full life:

> And we, with our unveiled faces reflecting like mirrors the brightness of the Lord, all grow brighter and brighter as we are turned into the image that we reflect; this is the work of the Lord who is Spirit (2 Cor 3:18).

Meditation

Place yourself on Mount Tabor as Jesus with Moses and Elijah is transfigured in glory. See Peter, James and John sharing in the transfiguring, Taboric light of Jesus.

"Rabbi, it is wonderful for us to be here" (Mk 9:2-13). At times we need to be alone on the mountain to experience the rays of God's uncreated energies of love penetrate, invade, bombard us from all sides. It is indeed wonderful to become light from Light.

But hear Jesus send you forth to become the light of your world (Mt 5:14-16). Respond joyfully to his commission to work through you to bring his glorious, resurrected presence into the world in order to transfigure it into his body by the light of love.

EIGHTH DAY

A Diaphanous World

The last day of your retreat is aimed at helping you make the transition from the top of the mountain, where you have met and conversed with the Blessed Trinity "as a man speaks with his friend" (Ex 33:11), back to the marketplace. You have seen your calling by God in Christ Jesus "to be holy and spotless, and to live through love in his presence" (Ep 1:4).

You are to become holy by the life you live in the world, God's created, material world from which you cannot escape without lessening your chances of becoming fully human. The world from which you must escape is the worldliness within your heart that sets up your unreal self in false independence of God.

Such worldliness within you is to be replaced by Christ risen and abiding in you: Christ is in you (Col 1:28). Contemplation is a state of finding God's loving presence easily in all things and of working creatively to cooperate in the Christification of the world.

I: The Indwelling Christ

There are some truths in the Christian faith that, if you were really to take them seriously and live them daily, would completely transform your life. One such central truth is that by grace Jesus Christ really lives within you. His glorious, resurrected, total person, God-man, abides inside of you with the Father through their Spirit.

Your entire life from birth to death is your search for your true self. You are made up of a bundle of selves. You have seen, in meditating on your brokenness, that because there is sin in your members (Rm 7:23), there are many *false* selves claiming to be your real self. You are incapable of healing your own state of disintegration. Only the Divine Physician, who possesses the fullness of life, can come and heal you. Only he, Jesus Christ, according to whose image and likeness you have been created (Gn 1:26), can fill you to your fullest potential.

A Life in Christ   It is through the Holy Spirit that you can fully know Jesus Christ and in his loving presence and in union with him find your true identity: "We know that he lives in us by the Spirit that he has given us" (1 Jn 3:24). By the love of God that is poured into your heart through the Spirit (Rm 5:5), you can come to a greater and greater awareness of your unique individuality in God's special love for you.

That Spirit "reaches the depths of everything, even the depths of God" (1 Cor 2:10). Through the power of Jesus' Spirit your hidden self can grow strong and Christ can live in your heart through faith so that you can grasp the breadth and length, the height and the depth of the love of Christ (Ep 3:16-18).

You grow into your true self, therefore, by dying to your unreal self so that in St. Paul's words, "You have died and now the life you have is hidden with Christ in God" (Col 3:3). St. Paul would tell you to find your *self* by "putting on Jesus Christ" (Ga 3:27; Ep 4:24) and by living "*in* Christ."

As we have seen, St. Paul uses the phrase "in Christ" very often to indicate "the mystery of Christ" (Ep 3:4) that he preached so ardently—an "incorporation" into Christ so intimate that Christians live no longer themselves but Christ Jesus lives *in* them (Ga 2:20). This is a real union and not merely a moral relationship. The life of Christ risen is to be shared intimately with you as the source of your true greatness and dignity.

You are in the most vital union with Christ who should operate in you as the principle of your every thought, word and deed. You share even now in Christ's own life in his glorious resurrectional presence. The Father sees you in him and loves you as a unique part of the total Christ.

> They are the ones he chose specially long ago and intended to become true images of his Son, so that his Son might be the eldest of many brothers (Rm 8:29-30).

To "put on Christ" is to become surrounded and penetrated by him. You have his being within you! Yet his presence, or better yet, your awareness of his presence, must grow as an embryo in a womb grows. St. Paul considered everything as rubbish, "if only I can have Christ and be given a place in him" (Ph 3:8). He labored zealously to fashion Jesus Christ in his faithful. "My children! I must go through the pain of giving birth to you all over again, until Christ is formed in you" (Ga 4:19).

The Christian Life   You can measure how much a Christian you are by your growth into the fullness of Christ. The more you are aware of him intimately abiding within you, the more you can open yourself to his loving guidance at each moment, and the more ready you will be to put to death anything that is un-Christlike or unbecoming a child of God in whom Christ dwells.

The Christian life does admit of a negative aspect of putting aside all that is "worldly" or self-centered. But such a task of vigilance and inner discipline is done with joy in the light of the union with Jesus risen. More positively your

181

Christian life becomes increasingly open to allow Jesus to direct your values and choices. He speaks commandments that are recognized by the Holy Spirit's infusion of knowledge.

To live in Christ is to love him. And love of Jesus is measured by seeking to make your will one with his. It is to become perfectly obedient to his wishes. How simply Jesus reduced the whole of the Christian life:

> If anyone loves me he will keep my word,
> and my Father will love him,
> and we shall come to him
> and make our home with him (Jn 14:23).

The sign, therefore, of whether you live in Christ is how well you keep his commandments, his directives to act lovingly in the context of your daily life: "If you keep my commandments, you will remain in my love. . . . This is my commandment: love one another as I have loved you" (Jn 15:10, 12).

Pray Always   We can understand how necessary it is to remain in God's indwelling presence if we are to be guided by that same indwelling presence. The success of our Christian living depends on our growth in awareness of God's presence as we experience his great love for us, empowering us through the Spirit of the risen Jesus to return love by living always to bring our will in conformity with his.

Jesus had spoken of "the need to pray continually and never lose heart" (Lk 18:1). St. Paul exhorts the early Christians:

> Be happy at all times; pray constantly; and for all things give thanks to God, because this is what God expects you to do in Christ Jesus (1 Th 5:17-18).

It is possible to pray always, not by concentrating on God, but by living in the reverence due to God as you wish

182

to please God at all times, as opposed to seeking your own desires. This is to fulfill the one great commandment to be true to God's word.

Turning Inward   How can you maintain a state of constant awareness of God's presence? Jan Ruysbroeck, the 14th-century Flemish mystic, teaches the necessity of inner attentiveness in three areas. The first is belief, through the movement of God's grace, that the Trinity dwells within and that, therefore, you can turn within and expect to find God dwelling within you. You believe that God is love and the three Persons are present and loving you as Father, Son and Holy Spirit. God has created you to share in God's family.

Secondly, you must be diligent to rid yourself of distracting images and all attachments of your heart to any created being, especially yourself. What a responsibility to guard your senses so as not to allow the useless and "worldly" (i.e., whatever feeds your spirit of self-absorption) to enter into your mind and carry you away from union with God! "Happy the pure in heart: they shall see God" (Mt 5:8).

Thirdly, there must be a free turning of your will toward God so that your whole being is directed, body, soul and spirit, to praise and glorify God.

In this way you can live in the name of Jesus and in his presence. He will live in your "heart" through increased faith, hope and love, given by the Spirit, and you will want at every moment, even when unable to "think" of God, to be one with the mind of Jesus: "We are those who have the mind of Christ" (1 Cor 2:16).

Return to the Marketplace   As you interiorly discover your *logos,* or unique personhood, in a conscious relationship of love to the *Logos*-made-flesh, Jesus Christ, you become free enough to break down your false posturing before God and your neighbors. You can let go of your aggressive attacks upon others or your weak withdrawal into "splendid isolation" and give your life in love to others. You come down from the mountain top of adoring your triune God to return to the marketplace where human life goes on in much multiplicity as well as in sordidness and brokenness.

But now you know that the Christ within you is also the same risen Jesus Christ inserted into every atom of matter. You willingly allow the Spirit of Jesus to send you among men and women to bind up their wounds and heal their hurts by the love of the Divine Physician, now come back to earth again, to heal all the sick if they believe that Jesus is being brought to them through your loving ministry.

There is a new power in your life now: the power of Christ that has gained mastery over your life. "And for anyone who is in Christ, there is a new creation; the old creation has gone, and now the new one is here" (2 Cor 5:17). And he sends you into the world with all his power (Mk 16:16). Becoming one with Christ in deep prayer, you have a new sense of oneness with all human beings, called by God to be a part of the body of Christ.

As you contemplate God everywhere present in his creation, both that which reflects his perfections and that which seemingly is absent to his beauty, you want to bring forth God's creative, healing power that makes you a "reconciler" (2 Cor 5:18) of the entire world to God.

You wish to share what material riches you have with your brothers and sisters who are in need. To the lonely and depressed, the anxious and the despondent, you want to be warm, loving hands of comfort. To those in sin you wish to be all things to win them to Christ. Caring concern is your watchword and privilege as you lovingly seek to serve all in need of whatever kind.

You understand that to love Jesus Christ is to serve his members:

My dear people,
let us love one another
since love comes from God
and everyone who loves is begotten by God and knows God.
Anyone who fails to love can never have known God,
because God is love. . . .
My dear people,
since God has loved us so much,
we too should love one another.
No one has ever seen God;
but as long as we love one another
God will live in us
and his love will be complete in us (1 Jn 4:7-12).

The authentic test of your union with Christ and your level of contemplation is the degree of love and humble service you show toward those who enter your life.

Meditation

Prayerfully ponder the words of Jesus that summarize this teaching in Jn 15:1-17. He is the vine; you the branch. Without him living in you, you are nothing but a dry and fruitless branch, fit only to be burned. But if you live in him and he is living in you, you will bring forth much fruit.

. . . and I commissioned you
to go out and to bear fruit,
fruit that will last. . . .
What I command you
is to love one another.

II: *You Are Church—The Body of Christ*

Dr. Carl Rogers, one of America's foremost psychiatrists, stresses how in every human being deep down in one's "innermost self" there is a nature that is forward-looking and societal.

One of the most revolutionary concepts to grow out of our clinical experience is the growing recognition that the innermost core of man's nature, the deepest layers of his personality, the base of his "animal nature," is positive in nature, is basically socialized, forward-moving, rational and realistic.

You have prayed in this retreat about God's eternal plan for all mankind, made according to God's very own image and likeness that is Jesus Christ. You have seen your own fulfillment to consist in a constant growth in conscious awareness of your oneness with Jesus Christ risen. As he lives within you and you freely surrender to be directed at all times by his Spirit, you begin to fulfill God's plan in your regard. You live with "ultimate concern," to quote Paul Tillich's phrase, and the results are evident in your life: love, peace, joy, gentleness, etc. These are the fruit of the Holy Spirit (Ga 5:22).

But love and gentleness, patience and kindness, cannot operate except in a society. All too often retreats end with the emphasis on the retreatant's spiritual life with the indwelling God, without so much as a movement outward toward a community. No one is ever "saved" alone, but the whole people of God is called into a oneness and that, you know in the New Testament, is the body of Christ, the church, the new people of God, the "holy people of Jesus Christ" (1 Cor 1:2). You are meant to find your fullness in the society that forms the body of Christ, with Christ as the head, directing each member through his Spirit in order that in the fruit of the Spirit the entire body will be built up and the whole of mankind will be reconciled to the Father through Jesus. It will be reconciled as a unity in love.

You cannot regard your own spiritual perfection without seeing it as living an authentic Christian life in an environment of love that is called the church of Christ. You are to receive direction from those in this body to whom

Christ has given the special charisms of teaching the word through their preaching with authority and of ministering the sacramental encounters between you and the risen, healing Jesus Christ. But you are to give also of your own charisms to build up this body and thus grow in praise, reverence and service in God's kingdom.

You Are Christ   From the first encounter with Jesus Christ, St. Paul met the Savior of the world as the cosmic Christ. He had set out to persecute the followers of the man named Jesus, who had been put to death in Jerusalem for blasphemously claiming, in substance, that he was God. But along the road to Damascus, Saul became Paul, and Jesus became for him the living Son of God, "the image of the unseen God, the first-born of all creation, for in him were created all things in heaven and on earth" (Col 1:15).

"Saul, Saul, why are you persecuting me?" (Ac 9:4). The haunting voice of Jesus seared Paul's being and was never to be forgotten. The implications of the Damascus vision would gradually become clearer to Paul through years of prayerful encounter with his Lord and in his preaching and writing to the early Christian communities, as he sought to build up the body of Christ, the church.

This church, for St. Paul and the early apostles of Jesus, was the community or brotherhood of Christian believers linked together by the bonds of faith and sacraments, especially baptism and the Eucharist. There was also the bond of obedience to the appointed bishops and presbyters who had been given Christ's authority to teach his word and minister his sacraments. This mystical body of Christ, the church, is a unique, real union between Christ the head and the individual members of whom you are a part. This union between Christ and you, as we have seen earlier, admits of an infinity of intimate growth. As you become healthier in the Spirit of love and in his charisms, you can let the love of Jesus' Spirit flow out into other persons, bringing healing love to the whole body.

Built into a Oneness by the Spirit   The Holy Spirit is the principle of the resurrection, the one "who raised Jesus from the dead (who) will give life to your own mortal bodies through his Spirit living in you" (Rm 8:11). The resurrection and glorification of the church, the building of it into one body, one faith (Ep 4:4), is brought about by the Spirit. As the Spirit animated Christ into a new, resurrectional life, so the same Spirit animates you and all other members, who receive the Spirit first in baptism, into the *new creation* that is the total Christ, now in pilgrimage, broken but constantly being healed by the Spirit's love, and which will one day enter into the full glory with Christ, its head.

The church is built up through the two missions of Jesus Christ and his Spirit. Jesus in his earthly life formed a nucleus for his church that would extend his physical, earthly existence into time and space until he would come at the end of time to lead his bride, the church, into final glory. This is the college of apostles to whom he gave authority to preach and teach his word and to minister his sacraments of healing to the broken ones of this world. This authority handed down through the successors of the apostles, the bishops, in union with the successor of St. Peter, the Pope of Rome, is a charism under the guidance of the Holy Spirit. There are other charisms different from the charisms of the visible authority of the hierarchical structure.

Of those charisms you have also received. The Spirit is constantly regenerating you into the fullness of Christ. This Spirit has been promised to you by Jesus Christ as the one to reveal to you all you need to know about Christ and his message. He will unite you in love with the other members of the body and give you the power to love all men and women throughout the entire world as your brothers and sisters.

Your Charisms   St. Paul speaks of the one Spirit in the body of Christ but a variety of gifts that he gives to the members in order to build up that body (1 Cor 12:4-11). You, as a unique member in the church, Christ's body, are important. As the life in Christ increases within you and you mature in him, you learn to forget yourself and live for the whole. You learn that you cannot love Jesus Christ and live in the trinitarian life unless you also are impelled by that same Spirit to love Jesus Christ in all his members. You have, therefore, a unique role to play that no one else on the face of the earth can fulfill exactly as you ought to fulfill it.

You can begin to see how your individual perfection is tied in with the perfection of the entire body of Christ. Your maturity in the Christian life is measured by your love for others shown in humble service. You are to aid in the building up of the body into the "perfect man," Christ. This is a process leading to greater consciousness of faith and infused knowledge of oneness with Christ. You are to grow into greater unity and stability in Christ in your own individual life and in your societal life within the church "by living the truth in love," to use St. Paul's phrase (Ep 4:15). We can paraphrase this as living an authentic Christian life in an environment of love. Faith accepts the truth, but the truth has to be lived in love (2 Th 2:12). Love makes the truth manifest. We live by the truth only when we are impelled to do so by love for God: "The truth will make you free" (Jn 8:32).

The whole Christian life must, therefore, be guided by this single aim: to live the truth in love, that is, to do at every moment God's will as read in your conscience, informed by grace, guiding you to act only and always out of love for God. Such acting out of love for God brings about the union of the members of the body with their head who is Christ (Ep 4:15). But such a union cannot be achieved, nor can we act out of love for God, except through Christ, the source of all true growth: "Cut off from me you can do nothing" (Jn 15:5).

In Christ and with Christ   All growth is from Christ, through and with him. Yet he gives growth only where there is a conscious effort on the individual's part to make contact with the source of supply. Paul uses the image drawn from the science of architecture: "Harmoniously joined and knit together." The side of one stone is worked so as to fit into the corresponding side of another stone. This means painstaking and exacting work to hew the rough edges, climaxed by drilling the unifying holes and pouring molten lead to bind the two stones together.

By exercising love toward others, you are to cut away any obstacles to the perfect unity that builds up the church as a new Temple in which dwells the God of Israel. Christ is the source of the supply of this unity among members built by actions done out of love. He produces a compact, unified mystical body, but only in the proportion that you and other members are in contact with Christ to receive from him his grace and are ready to transmit this life-grace through service or love to fellow members.

Love proved by action is the propulsion that moves a Christian toward Christ. But the more you, as a single member, love Christ through the love of your neighbor, the more the whole body becomes "full" of the love of Christ.

Brokenness in the Body of Christ   The church is the bride of Christ, holy and spotless, yet it is made up of sinful men and women. You are in Christ, but you are not completely given to him. The church is made up of pilgrims like yourself who must, individually and as a group, stretch out to become always more and more Christ. The church is as broken as the individual members are broken. It is as healthy as you, a given member, are healthy and can bring to the sick members of the body the life-giving power of Christ's love, his Spirit.

You go from this retreat praising God for his goodness to you in having set you free. But tomorrow you will discover new areas that hold you in bondage. Jesus is your Lord and master. Yet you always hold the possibility within yourself of turning away from him and making yourself, as Eve did, your own master and god. As you can individually recognize your own pilgrim-condition and your need of Jesus Christ to become your ever-present healer, you can cry out in realistic tension: "Come, Lord Jesus — Marana tha!" and "Thank you, Lord, for having set me free!"

Like the broken disciples of Jesus who betrayed him and ran away from their crucified Savior, you can hope that the risen Jesus will continue to release his Spirit in you and transform you little by little from the harlot-wife of Hosea into the faithful bride of Christ. And as you are transformed into Christ, so the body of Christ, the church, will also move to that day when Jesus will claim it as his pure and spotless spouse.

Meditation

Pray out the texts of St. Paul that teach the truth that you are Christ's body:
1. Rm 12:4-5.
2. 1 Cor 12:12-30.
3. Ep 4:10-16.
4. Ep 1:22-23.
5. Jn 15:1-17.

191

ALONE WITH THE ALONE

III: *Finding God in All Things*

We come to the end of the retreat. A retreat, however, should really never end but always, each day, be a beginning as we seek to live more fully the Christian mystery. It is a call to grow in contemplating God in all things. And, as we discover God present in more events of our lives by the living of our baptism of death to self and a new sharing in the resurrection of Jesus, we will let him live in our hearts through faith. We will be planted in love and grow to be "filled with the utter fullness of God" (Ep 3:18-19).

We have seen how contemplation, as taught in scripture and the writings of the Greek Fathers, develops on two levels. As we purify our hearts, we intuitively grasp, by the Spirit's infused faith, hope and love, God's Logos in each creature and in each event. Abiding in God's Logos we are led progressively into the trinitarian family of Father, Son and Spirit, living within us and loving us into our unique personhood. We also are able to discover the same one Trinity in three persons loving around us and acting in all creatures.

The following consideration is given as a summary of how you may go forth in your daily life and grow in the very life of the Trinity into becoming a greater contemplative. It is a vision of God's immanent and loving presence in all things so that you may live always "planted in love and built on love."

Degrees of Presence   God is love (1 Jn 4:8). Love is always a movement outwardly from the depths of a person's being to share his or her being with another. It is a movement of self-communication unto union where two finally become one, united in love and yet aware of their unique differences.

To express love that first stirs within God's "heart" or deepest level of his being, God moves himself in actions of communication. Love needs an external expression of self-giving in creative action.

But such creative action admits of several levels of self-giving or being "present" to the one loved.

1. God wishes to be present to you in the created gifts that he gives you. He reflects his beauty and perfections in the limited perfections of his creatures. What should be your response to God's presence as giver of all gifts? At all times to thank him and praise him: "Bless Yahweh, my soul!" (Ps 104:1). "Praise Yahweh, my soul!" (Ps 146:1).

2. God wishes to be even more present to you by being *inside* of each gift. As you touch each creature given to you by God, you come into his loving presence. What is our response to God's omnipresence in all things? "Where could I go to escape your spirit? Where could I flee from your presence?" (Ps 139:7). The response called for is one of reverence. As you touch each created gift, you touch God's holy presence. This place is holy! You move in an atmosphere of reverent awe at God's all-pervasive, loving presence everywhere.

3. But God wishes still more to be present to you in his self-giving love. He does this not merely by being present in each creature but by acting out of loving service to make you happy. God is most present to you as he is working constantly in each moment and in each creature (Jn 5:17) to allow you to receive him in loving union. What is your response? Be present, not only by praising and reverencing him in all things, but by working and serving his holy will in all that you do.

Praise, reverence and service to God constitute a continued gift of yourself in loving surrender back to God who gives himself so completely to you at all times. This is where love is contemplation. Contemplation is, therefore, a state of being present to God in self-giving so that your whole being is constantly offering itself in love as a pleasing gift to him.

Thanksgiving for God's Gifts   You can best review the gifts of God by reviewing the closest things to you, i.e., yourself, your being brought into existence, all the gifts of nature, the gifts of redemption and sanctification bringing you into God's own life.

1. *The gift of yourself.* We do tend to take ourselves for granted. Reflect: There was a time when you did not exist, but there will never be another time when you will not exist. Yet in the mind of God, in his love for you, you always existed, for he had an idea in his mind that was you from all eternity. There was never a time when God was not thinking of you. He cannot love you more tomorrow than he loves you today and has loved you yesterday: "I have loved you with an everlasting love, so I am constant in my affection for you" (Jr 31:3). Of all the billions of creatures possible that never saw the light of existence, you were chosen by God to *be,* to exist. And when in time he brought you forth, when on that certain day you became a human being, when this divine thought of God became incarnated in you, you were destined by God to go on living with his own eternity. You are never to cease to exist.

And his only purpose is love, to share his goodness, his happiness with you. How good and unselfish is God toward you! What gratitude should there be for the gift of existence that makes your life so uniquely full of meaning, God-meaning, compared to other creatures destined by God only to be an aid for you to attain eternal life.

Ponder prayerfully all the gifts of God wrapped up in your creation: your faculties of intellect, will, imagination, memory; your senses, so marvelous, so intricate and mysterious. You are made in God's image and likeness through your ability to think, know and love. Think of your health and the many years that you have enjoyed it. If you suddenly realized that some wealthy person has for years thought of you, loved you and has been sending you mysterious gifts, would you not want to know what he is like and to thank him? God has been doing this for you every moment of your existence. The more you realize the genuineness and depth of his love for you, the nearer you are brought to a point of wanting sincerely to love him in return.

2. *Gifts of nature.* Here the list is endless — all the creatures that God has generously poured out into your life just for you to see them and to glorify him. The flowers, trees, birds, animals, the beauties of each new season, sun, moon, stars, mountains, lakes, oceans, a world to please you, to teach you about God and his perfections.

You share the above gifts with others in some way or other. But there are gifts that you alone have received. At least, no one else has received from God this or that type of gift in the same degree you have. Think of your personality and its strengths, your talents, the many friends who have been gifts of love fashioning you into the person you are, so different from anyone else. Think of your blood relatives, especially any brothers and sisters. Are they successful, happy, compared to the success and happiness that you possess? See how God has heaped gifts upon you and never tires of continuing to give you his choicest gifts. And all these are mere symbols of the real gift he wants to give you, if only you would open your arms and accept him, in this life and for all eternity.

3. *Supernatural Gifts.* Ponder God's personal, involving love in sharing his life with you by calling you to be his chosen child by grace (Jn 1:12). Think of God's gift of his Son, Jesus Christ: "God loved the world so much that he gave his only Son, so that everyone who believes in him may not be lost but may have eternal life" (Jn 3:16).

You have received the gift of faith and have been baptized a Christian. Thank God for the gift of Christian parents and teachers, friends and priests, who have developed that gift of faith. How many times have you received the sacrament of reconciliation and had your sins wiped away with God's merciful forgiveness? How many times have you been privileged to receive Jesus in the Eucharist and to attend the divine liturgy?

Jesus is continually releasing the Holy Spirit in your heart and bestowing upon you his particular charisms to build up his church. In that Spirit what precious moments of happiness and strength you received as the Spirit powerfully prayed within you (Rm 8:26-27).

Ask yourself, "What is my response, my return to God for all he has given me?" Will you just go on receiving his gifts like a selfish child? Will you make no return to such burning love of God who wishes to call you into the deepest union with him?

"Take, O Lord, and receive, all my memory, my understanding, my will. Everything I have is yours, Lord. Take it as it belongs to you. But receive it as my personal gift back to You. Give me only your love and your grace and I shall be rich enough and shall not ask for anything more." God's love is God himself. It is his very being. "Just give me that and I think I shall be rich enough! Give me your grace!" That is God's uncreated energies of love coming to you through his Holy Spirit and the glorified Jesus Christ. You are asking that you feel within yourself the current of God's divine love in every gift and that you can return yourself to him in a song of praise that becomes equivalent to the sacrifice of yourself totally to God at every moment.

Reverence for God's Presence in All Things   Try to see that God is not content merely with giving himself to you in an extrinsic way. He wishes to be more present to you by being present in the very gifts he gives you. God not only creates the gifts he wishes you to receive, but he also personally presents them to you. He remains present in every gift as though he shouts out to you: "Here I am, not far from you, for all things move and have their being in me" (cf. Ac 17:28).

Everything you touch can be the sacred point of contacting God's inside presence. Everything shouts out that God is within, wishing to give himself more completely to you as you open up to his inner presence in all creatures. The logical conclusion to God's presence in all creatures is that you should want to be present to him by reverence. Everything you touch this day should be a sacred moment of consecration as you unite yourself with the presence of God everywhere. This thing and this place are holy. No longer do the material things that enter into your moment-by-moment existence take you away from God's presence but now you intuit God's loving presence inside all things.

Your return to God's great love for his being present in all things is the reverence you show as you handle all creation, especially as you meet other human beings, for God is truly here!

God's Working Presence in All Things   God is a lover different from human lovers, who give a gift which is exterior to them. God is working in all his gifts, giving of himself as a sign of his love. Creation is an ongoing process and God is patiently working from inside each creature in the potentiality he has poured into that finite creature. He is the ground of being directing all creatures to their full actuality.

Think of how God has been working for you in his ongoing creation. From the very beginning of time, he has been creating the world, the heavens and the earth, directing the laws of nature for millions of years, to prepare for you a pleasant abode on this earth. See how he works in the wonderful evolution of various plant and animal life to give you such a variety of food and clothing. Think of how much labor and time go into the preparation of a piece of ordinary meat that you eat at table. What a tremendous effort on the part of God to show you his loving presence in his giving of himself to you, in his working for you.

God wants you to find him also in the most ordinary work of your life. Think of the special manner in which God participates in the suffering and death of Jesus, his Son, giving you a model so that you also may find God easily in your sufferings and in all your works that may cause you a struggle. See that God is working with you, as Jesus during all his human life discovered his Father working in all things, and as he himself sought to work along with the Father (Jn 5:17).

Your response is to do everything in your daily work for love of God but now with the realization that God is within you and in the material over which you are working. The two of you are working to fashion the total Christ, the body made up of this material world, which has its fullness of being in the Logos of God.

Meditation

Reflect on Acts 17:16-28.

In the presence of the living Trinity abiding within you, stretch out your empty hands and humbly ask God to fill them with his energies of love. Beg him to use your weaknesses in order that his glory, his *Shekinah,* may appear to you in each event. Cry out in pain that the full Jesus Christ be brought forth in glory. Offer your hands and lips to be channels of the healing power of Jesus Christ among his people again. God is at the heart of matter. And matter is moving, by your prayerful contemplation of God and yourself in loving service, toward spirit.

Learn that your life is to praise God in his gifts; be present to God in reverence as you discover him in all things; above all, work with him who is working inside of each event, that Christ be brought forth, and so that you with the risen Jesus and his Spirit of love can be a *praise, reverence* and *service* out of returned love to him who is love itself.

198

Mary in Glory

It is good at the end of a retreat to remain standing on the mountain top and look far into the future to the final end of your life and the life of this world. What will you be like when you die? How you answer about your far future will determine your attitude toward life now. For as you make your choices now, so you will be in the life to come. A retreat should stimulate you greatly, not only to ask ultimate questions, but, hopefully, to seek their answers by the way you choose to live in the present moment.

To review your retreat you might ask such questions as the following: "Why do I act? Is it in order to live? What does it mean for me to live? What is the test of a good, human life? After I die, what happens? Shall I really go on living, and in what shape or form?" You need to become self-reflective about the purpose of your life and its direction so that you can live your present gift of life in the most meaningful way.

You have already meditated on Christ risen. You hope in the resurrection of your body, and through you and other living members of his body, the church, the material universe also can become part of the glorified body of Christ. Because Jesus is risen and you already are a part of his risen body, you, too, can even now live in the coming of the resurrection. He is "the first-fruits of all who have fallen asleep" (1 Cor 15:20). As Christ through his human body touched all men, so by the resurrection of his human body, our bodies and the whole universe have the possibility of being reoriented to God. This reorientation will lead eventually to a full resurrection in the Spirit.

Christ risen touches this material world by giving us the Spirit. The indwelling Spirit imparts to you the life of God through the divinely uncreated energies of love, but he exerts his influence on your body as well. "And if the Spirit of him who raised Jesus from the dead is living in you, then he who raised Jesus from the dead will give life to your own mortal bodies through his Spirit living in you" (Rm 8:11).

The Assumption of Mary   In the month of August Catholics and Orthodox celebrate one of the most ancient feasts of Mary, the Mother of God—her assumption into glory. Although this belief in her glorification is not found explicitly in holy scripture, nevertheless, it draws its strength from the reflection of the church over centuries, as Christians ponder Mary's greatness: she is the archetype of the church and of individual Christians who make up the church.

The church throughout the centuries pondered prayerfully two texts that touch by analogy the assumption of Mary. In Genesis 3:15, the seed of the woman is to crush the head of the serpent and strike its heel. Mary is the New Eve, bringing forth Christ, the New Adam; and both he and she would triumph over evil. In the book of Revelation (12:1-17) a woman is clothed with the sun, standing on the moon, with twelve stars on her head for a crown. She is rescued from the pursuing devil by receiving a huge pair of eagle's wings to escape from the serpent into the desert.

Through apocryphal stories, homilies of the church fathers, liturgical hymns and prayers, church tradition gives us the basic belief of the church that Mary, the Mother of

God, has been raised incorruptible, body and soul, total person, and is now in glory in heaven. Here is a typical early Christian hymn as sung in the Byzantine liturgy for the feast of the assumption:

> In thee, O spotless Maiden,
> > The bounds of nature are overstepped:
> Childbearing is virginal;
> > Death is but a pledge of life.
> After giving birth, thou art a maiden,
> > After death, alive.
> O Godbearer,
> > Thou dost save us, thy heritage,
> Unceasingly!

On November 1, 1950, Pope Pius XII declared as infallible dogma the truth, taught and believed in the church, both East and West for many centuries, that Mary upon her physical death on this earth, was glorified in heaven, body and soul. We Christians believe God has done to Mary what he will do to us if we die in the Lord. We believe that our whole person, body and soul, will be raised to a new level of existence. God created us to be "whole" persons. The whole person, the biblical, physical body-man in death does not experience a separation of body and soul. There is an end to our immersion in a lower stage of our evolutionary development.

But as we celebrate Mary's assumption into glory, we profess that we too will enter into a body-soul-spirit resurrection. Mary is the leading member of the body of Christ. She is tied closely to the head, Jesus Christ, who is risen in glory. As she, all her lifetime, died to self and became full of grace by living in faith, hope and love, so was she always entering into a progressive sharing of the glory of her Son as she became more united with him in her humble submission to God's word. Her future glory was dependent upon her daily choices to die to selfishness and to rise to allow God's word to be done completely in her life. She grew each day as a whole person.

Jesus is risen in glory and Mary is the one who most shares in his resurrection because she died all her life to let Jesus live. If Mary is, therefore, the image and beginning of the church, is it not possible to believe that, as she is now in glory, so in a similar way are the saints, who with her form the heavenly church? It is the whole heavenly church, the body of Christ in glory, that is exalted by Jesus Christ's Spirit and is the prototype of what all of us who make up the earthly church will be in the future, when we too shall pass, as Mary and the other saints passed through death and entered into their glory, by participating in the resurrection of their head, Jesus Christ.

Our Hope   The glory of Mary and the glory of the saints is the glory of the body of Christ, the heavenly Jerusalem, the new creation. The heavenly church, no longer in pilgrimage, is in glory, and Mary is the holiest of all the members of that glorified body of Christ. We stretch out in hope to reach also the state of glory that they enjoy. The woman clothed with the sun is both Mary and the heavenly church. The great sign is Mary as the church.

We also are a part of that church, the body of Christ. What we believe God's Spirit has accomplished in Mary and in the other members of the heavenly church, we eagerly await to be accomplished in us. Our hope through Christ's revelation is that not only our soul, but our bodies, our total persons, will be joined to the resurrectional life of the living Savior.

But as Mary grew each day of her earthly existence in fullness of grace as she died to self and rose to a new life in God, so we also are even now entering into a new sharing in the resurrectional body of Christ. Death is resurrection,

202

even now, as we allow Jesus to be Master and Lord in our life. And that resurrection, which will await the fullness to come at the end of this world, is already being experienced both in our life and in the church as we share even now in his death-resurrection. The end of our life ultimately, and even now in each choice that we make, is not death but glorification. The church is Jesus Christ extended into time. We are a part of the church and are in glory as Mary is to the degree that we die to our selfishness. What happens to Mary through her process of death-resurrection is happening to us. By living out of love for God and neighbor, as Mary did all her lifetime, we come to live our baptism and put on Christ.

A Cosmic Glorification   But if our material being will reach its completion by a transformation and "ascension" from this earthly existence to an "incorruptible" one, our Christian faith expresses the hope that the whole cosmos will be transfigured into a "new creation." It is the glorified Christ that associates himself as mediator in bringing the universe to its appointed completion in order that God may be everything to everyone and everything (1 Cor 15:28). God's will is to gather all creation both in heaven and on earth under one head, Christ (Ep 1:10). Christ has complete primacy and dominion over the cosmic universe through his death and resurrection. The whole created world is to become a part of the one Christ, the heavenly Jerusalem, fashioning his body into a glory to the Father as he contemplates what St. Paul beautifully describes: "There is only Christ; he is everything and he is in everything" (Col 3:11).

Mary and the other saints, those in glory already sharing in the resurrection of Christ, their head, seek constantly to share their happiness and joy by interceding for us on earth. Their oneness with Christ impels them to go among the broken ones of this earth and to bind up their wounds out of love for Christ and out of love for the potential members of his body to become parts of themselves and thus add to their fuller glory.

Mary and the other saints, our glorified brothers and sisters, make it possible for us to hope for a share of their glory when we, by God's grace, shall also become with them a part of the heavenly church, the body of Christ in full glory. Then we will understand the prophetic words of St. Paul:

> May the God of our Lord Jesus Christ, the Father of glory, give you a spirit of wisdom and perception of what is revealed, to bring you to full knowledge of him. May he enlighten the eyes of your mind so that you can see what hope his call holds for you, what rich glories he has promised the saints will inherit and how infinitely great is the power that he has exercised for us believers. This you can tell from the strength of his power at work in Christ, when he used it to raise him from the dead and to make him sit at his right hand, in heaven, far above every Sovereignty, Authority, Power or Domination or any other name that can be named, not only in this age but also in the age to come. He has put all things under his feet, and made him, as the ruler of everything, the head of the Church, which is his body, the fullness of him who fills the whole creation (Ep 1:17-23).